Determination of Value

Founded in 1807, John Wiley & Sons is the oldest independent publishing company in the United States. With offices in North America, Europe, Asia, and Australia, Wiley is globally committed to developing and marketing print and electronic products and services for our customers' professional and personal knowledge and understanding.

The Wiley Corporate F&A series provides information, tools, and insights to corporate professionals responsible for issues affecting the profitability of their company, from accounting and finance to internal controls and performance management.

Determination of Value

Guidance on Developing and Supporting Credible Opinions

FRANCISCO ROSILLO

WILEY

Library of Congress Cataloging-in-Publication Data

Rosillo, Francisco, 1951–
 Determination of value : appraisal guidance on developing and supporting a credible opinion / Francisco Rosillo.
   pages cm. — (Wiley corporate F&A series)
 Includes index.
 ISBN 978-1-118-28789-7 (cloth); ISBN 978-1-118-33149-1 (ePub);
 ISBN 978-1-118-33374-7 (ePDF); ISBN 978-1-118-33486-7 (eMobi)
  1. Valuation. 2. Corporations—Valuation. I. Title.
  HG4028.V3R5825 2013
  658.15--dc23
                                                          2013004414
Printed in the United States of America

10 9 8 7 6 5 4 3 2 1

*This book is dedicated to my friend and colleague,
Mr. William J. Brown, Esq., a true scholar of the law, whose
explanations, views, and perspectives of how legal reasoning affects
decision makers, litigants, and the ultimate outcome of legal
actions have helped many of his peers.*

*This book is also dedicated to my wife and five children,
who have relentlessly listened to my incantations on
the subject matter of this book and yet continued to encourage me
to write this manuscript.*

Contents

Chapter 8: Enhancing the Integrity of Your Opinion 149

Chapter 9: Reviewing the Work of Others 169

Chapter 10: The Journey Continues 189

x ▪ Contents

Preface

JUST THE FACTS, MA'AM."

I am still reminded of Sergeant Joe Friday from the TV show *Dragnet*, who would regularly proclaim so. Alas, for much simpler times now gone when just the facts were enough to make a decision. Have you ever wondered why stakeholders and decision makers turn to "experts" in a given field for opined conclusions to incorporate into a given decision-making process? Or why so-called expert opinions are needed at all?

Every single day the landscape of commercial transactions and social interactions becomes ever more complex. Against this background, whenever issues arise, decision makers are presented with difficult, if not nearly impossible, facts and circumstances to navigate in search for a truth on those matters before them. Decision makers turn to those who hold themselves as experts to help them navigate the vast amounts of information and facts to be considered.

No matter the subject matter or field of endeavor, from law enforcement, health care, law, engineering, or the appraisal disciplines, the continuing reliance on expert opinions is likely to increase; achieving an understanding of these dynamics is an important endeavor for anyone who must come before others to present a conclusion or opinion on those issues at hand.

This book attempts to dissect the dynamics I have experienced in the discipline of opining before others. Over the past two decades, I have come to the realization that the discipline of opining is best understood and practiced when a practitioner comes to the sober conclusion that opining is a search for a truth among an unresolved, and many times poorly defined, set of facts and circumstances. However, opining itself does not represent a truth over any given matter. And so, as one uncovers the transcendental elements underpinning the processes affecting the search for a given truth, the ability to effectively, precisely, and concisely state one's opinion can be materially expanded. In the chapters that follow, we will travel on a journey, a familiar journey in many aspects, yet traveled from different perspectives.

- Chapter 1 discusses the nature of the problems facing opining individuals.
- Chapter 2 presents and analyzes a practical definition of credibility.
- Chapter 3 lays out the criteria for a well-defined analytical process.
- Chapter 4 presents a different opining attitude: pyramids, not castles.
- Chapter 5 examines the necessary elements of the Credibility Pyramid.
- Chapter 6 discusses how to develop, report, and present opined results.
- Chapter 7 discusses how reasonableness tests are an important part of the opining process.
- Chapter 8 suggests steps to enhance the integrity of opinions.
- Chapter 9 introduces a simple approach when reviewing the work of others.
- Chapter 10 offers suggestions on continuing your personal journey with newfound enhanced awareness.

Acknowledgments

I WISH TO ACKNOWLEDGE MY FRIEND and colleague, Mr. Howard A. Lewis, former executive director of the Institute of Business Appraisers, retired program manager for the Internal Revenue Service, National Engineering Program, and author of *Business Valuation Standards of the Internal Revenue Service*. Howard's advice and guidance were always welcomed and most productive.

CHAPTER ONE

The Problem

A S A CENTRIST SOCIETY, WE live in a world of middle-of-the-road solutions, that is based on some ungrounded concept that "splitting the baby" somehow brings about equitable results, a world where many decision makers embrace the premise of "splitting the baby" as an acceptable alternative, if for no other reason than out of sheer frustration.

 ## IN SEARCH OF A TRUTH

Circa 287–200 BC, Archimedes was so sure of his discovery regarding the relationship between weight and water displacement that he ignored his nakedness as he ran down the streets of then Syracuse, overcome by what he regarded as the truth of an issue before him. Similarly, during biblical times, King Solomon faced competing claims from two mothers, each claiming custody of a newborn. Faced with such a dilemma, King Solomon had to make a decision in search of a truth. Unlike the folklore derived from this story, King Solomon never intended to split the baby in half; instead, it was a device to get to the truth of the matter. King Solomon's application of intellectual rigor to his analysis of

the facts before him has become a symbol of wisdom and analytical thought. He concluded that the real mother would never allow her newborn to be sacrificed and would instead give up her claim in order to save the baby. Perhaps the most interesting parallels between Archimedes' and King Solomon's experiences and the subject matter in this book are the application of an analytical process, together with the exercise of intellectual rigor.

And so, instead of seeking middle-of-the road solutions, when it comes to matters involving the proffering of opinions, such as situations involving the determination of value, decision makers and stakeholders should carefully weigh any opined facts or issues proffered before them.

Seeking middle-of-the-road solutions is tantamount to saying that the good, the bad, and the ugly can somehow be suitably reconciled on the journey toward achieving credible results. To remedy this chaotic state of affairs, opining individuals need to follow a well-defined and articulated analytical process resulting from the application of intellectual rigor in order to get to the truth of a given matter, as did King Solomon and Archimedes.

Decision makers' frustration over the lack of foundation of the matters presented before them is real and should not be underestimated. In some instances, this frustration with a given decision-making process can create an overwhelming sense of uncertainty.

These high levels of uncertainty tend to turn into a perception of higher risks, whether true or imagined, which, when translated into economic decision making, may ultimately result in demands for higher investment returns.

And then one day, circa 2008, we abruptly awakened to the prospects of a worldwide recession and economic pandemonium, events that created an environment that now demands a more insightful view of many economic events surrounding us.

Since then, many have started asking, How could this worldwide economic mayhem have happened so quickly? How could financial and economic indices have changed so quickly and by so much, in scope as well as magnitude, in such a short time?

This seems in complete contradiction to the proposition that the age of technology has provided us with an information world where disclosure and transparency should be readily available on any one issue, on a real-time, ad hoc basis.

Perhaps the warnings were always there, yet were hidden from most of us by the large amount of unreliable information advanced by conflict-ridden individuals, proffering self-serving opinions and points of view, and aided, in many instances, by the ever-hungry 24-hour media, always searching for content to pitch to their audiences.

These warnings were also present in the widely accepted but flawed propositions proffered by self-serving individuals, held as worthy of belief by many, who never stopped to consider the credibility of these proposed views. Which, by the way, regardless of venue—whether appraisal disciplines, law, politics, finance, economics, health care, engineering, or law enforcement—were equally acted on and accepted as dogma by many, albeit challenged by some, but to no avail, until it was too late.

In addition, I submit to you that as a centrist society, we have gotten used to accepting middle-of-the-road solutions in hopes that the middle-of-the-road approach to decision making can lead the way to a correct outcome.

Such conventional wisdom also seems to say that if you average a high and a low finding, the result points to the correct number, with no further consideration of the underpinning issues and without considering the consequences of flawed analyses.

Perhaps if an objective means to assess the credibility of these views had been in common use, the economic pandemonium could have been averted or, at least, managed better. Still today, most individuals, when presented with two or more opposing views on a subject matter, tend to choose a middle ground, an average, if you will, rather than pausing to soberly determine the degree of credibility attaching to each of the presented views.

Sometimes, averages or middle-of-the-road propositions may work, yet in instances where the response to an issue or a problem entails an "opined" result, especially one requiring qualitative, as well as quantitative, analysis, choosing a middle-of-the-road position may unknowingly lead to the least desirable outcome. Add to this mix today's litigious social environment, and you can quickly understand how stakeholders and decision makers, as users of the work products of opposing opining individuals, often find themselves highly frustrated. Perhaps this high level of frustration ultimately leads decision makers to resort to these averaging responses, simply due to lack of a means to assess the credibility of the foundation on which proffered opinions are presented.

To understand the profound and transcendental impact of these issues, which go well beyond any appraisal or valuation process, one should also consider that in business and economic decision-making endeavors, frustration is a reflection of uncertainty.

Uncertainty, in turn, is an outcome of perceived risks.

If you subscribe to the generally accepted view that capital is risk averse, it follows that capital formation is not likely to occur when frustrations and perceived risks, whether real or not, exist unresolved in the minds of decision makers and stakeholders.

Economic uncertainty, fueled by perceived risks, can ultimately lead to economic stagnation or, at the very least, contribute to an inability to grow an economy in a healthy and prosperous fashion.

On a personal level, while in pursuit of a decision about a problem before you, you may find yourself surrounded by a sea of information and ever-growing requirements that continue to gather around you, and you can't help but wonder, how are you going to keep your head above the water's edge?

 ## THE ASSURANCE EXPERT

Is there any reason to be optimistic? Yes!

"Why?" you may rightly ask.

One of the fixes, I submit, is the birth of the "assurance expert."

This new breed of expert helps stakeholders understand risk—risk as defined in their own endeavors. For example, risk to an investor would relate to risk reward and risk aversion; to a health-care practitioner, risk would relate to the probability of an adverse outcome; and to an engineer, risk may relate to the likelihood of a catastrophic failure. In the determination of value, an assurance expert may be a valuation analyst performing a qualitative review of another analyst's work product, with the intended objective of assessing the credibility and suitability of such a work product, in light of the purpose and engagement objectives supporting the value to be opined.

This new breed of expert will be well schooled in his or her own disciplines and adept at assessing credibility in his or her own work product, as well as in the work of other experts.

The assurance expert will be in fact an "expert's expert," whose work product and findings will help stakeholders navigate through their respective decision-making processes. Transparency, accountability, informed judgment, adequate disclosures—all of these elements will be arrows in the quiver of the assurance expert.

He or she will be jointly appointed by claimants and respondents, plaintiffs and defendants, and some day by the tribunals and/or the decision makers themselves.

The assurance expert will become a reality in our social infrastructure, if for no other reason than because of the dictum that calls for capital to be driven to sectors where transparency is available. In addition to the simple and brutal consequence that the economic survival of our society will demand it.

Capital is driven to economic sectors where the presence of transparency and accountability fosters a stable and predictable environment, where individuals and business concerns can transact and prosper.

This simple thesis points to the proposition that poor decision making increases the cost of capital and makes a society less efficient in the use of its resources.

Many of these issues could be resolved if credibility assessments could be made, so that decision-making processes that are presently embroiled in frustrating considerations of facts and circumstances and replete with uncertainty could be swiftly and efficiently resolved.

At such a point, one can begin to appreciate the importance of decision making based on credible assessments, because it would help to

- Ease efficient decision-making processes.
- Lower risk, by helping to eliminate doubts and perceived risks.
- Attract and stimulate capital formation.
- Create growth opportunities for economic participants.

Now, let's see how all of this comes together by way of a simple illustration.

Suppose that you are about to realize your lifetime goal of owning a chain of sporting goods stores. As you are getting ready for your grand opening, two sales representatives come to visit you, each claiming to be correct, to sell you a newly invented widget.

Each sales representative offers you his or her self-serving "opinion" of the retail-selling price of this newly invented widget.

Sales Rep A claims a retail selling price of $10 per widget.
Sales Rep B claims a retail selling price of $30 per widget.

You, as the store owner, stand perplexed, perhaps even frustrated, facing such widely different opinions, and after a period of reflection, you select a selling price of $20 per widget.

Conventional wisdom led you to choose a middle-of-the-road solution, especially when faced with no other set of facts to consider, probably due to the lack of data on this newly invented widget. This type of decision-making process happens every day, in judicial settings, corporate suites, colleges, universities, government, and so on.

So, what could be wrong with this form of conventional decision-making wisdom?

You, as the store owner, could have demanded to know the basis for each sales rep's retail selling price assumptions and the methodologies that were used to determine the results and then proceeded to determine the relevance of the opined amounts given, in order to assess which set of assumptions exhibited the highest level of credibility, before making your decision.

As the store owner, you are interested in maximizing the capital invested in the chain of stores, and you should be searching for the optimal answer:

What is the widget retail selling price at which you could sell the greatest number of widgets at the highest-yielding margin?

By simply taking an average, you may be limiting your ability to obtain a higher profit margin and, if incorrect, you equally run the risk of overestimating the selling price and thus limiting your ability to sell more widgets at the highest possible selling margins.

In a courtroom setting, this could be a jury choosing a middle ground after considering the testimony of two experts, resulting in an equally flawed solution, as in the case of the store owner, or perhaps rewarding a proponent who is otherwise lacking in credibility, while punishing the credible proponent.

The judicial system, overloaded with claims, many from less-than-reliable sources, tries to stay afloat by codifying requirements in the judicial rules to require gate-keeping roles of the judges in our courts.

Yet despite the judicial system's honest efforts at keeping junk science from distorting the matters before it, the results, I submit, are less than desirable in many instances and frequently are derived via a process that lacks a well-reasoned approach. The outcome then leads to a state of affairs where intellectual rigor has often been replaced by a manipulation of facts and circumstances, at times aided by a skillful understanding of how form can ultimately win over substance, regardless of purpose.

The unfairness, maybe even the insanity, of this set of circumstances and outcomes is due to the use of a simple averaging of opinions.

In these instances, decision makers are clearly, albeit unknowingly, acknowledging that each side of an argument is equally correct. This implies a closeness of the presented facts and circumstances that is then proposed to be bridged by application of the averaging wisdom, when in fact no such closeness or similarity may actually exist.

This may be tantamount to saying that the good, the bad, and the ugly can somehow be suitably reconciled on the journey toward achieving credible results.

When opinions matter, the selection of an average may lead to the least desirable of all outcomes, resulting in inequity, rather than fairness—an outcome yielding an incorrect course of action, versus the most efficient and productive one.

By now, you can appreciate the importance of credibility as a crucial factor in any decision-making process and how lack of an objective tool to assess credibility has led to poor decision making, thus increasing the cost of capital and resulting in a less efficient use of resources.

The problem-solving processes discussed in the chapters that follow are a lot less complicated than you might think and are indeed easy to apply—once you reach the proper level of awareness. These problem-solving techniques consist of the application of a qualitative methodology to assess the credibility of results presented by an opining individual and are intended to help stakeholders and decision makers understand risk—risk as defined in their own endeavors.

These problem-solving techniques can also assist opining individuals and decision makers in identifying and assessing the presence or the lack of transparency, accountability, and, ultimately, credibility of matters before them.

CREDIBILITY IS NOT SYNONYMOUS WITH TRUTH

A major issue addressed in the following chapters deals with the proposition for a definition of *credibility* and introduces an analytical framework for understanding and assessing credibility, as a self-standing and unique process to be achieved by any opining individuals.

The terms *credible* and *credibility*, along with their variations, are used in descriptive ways in many settings, laws, regulations, sets of criteria, and so on, yet an operational definition of *credibility*, with its own conceptual framework, has not gained general acceptability.

I submit that credibility points the way to a truth; however, *credibility* and *truth* are not the same thing and therefore should not be used interchangeably.

In today's world, any given truth must be sorted out, ideally, from a set of credible opinions, facts, and analyses offered for consideration. A simple case in point: One could easily refer to many instances in our everyday lives where certain beliefs are held by groups of individuals, who may feel those beliefs are credible, yet they are not considered to constitute a truth to the rest of society. Credibility is part of the path to a truth. The intent here is not to cast credibility in a relative fashion that can be shaped in any way or form to achieve a particular or perceived need.

 ## WHERE DO WE GO FROM HERE?

The treatises presented in the following chapters are intended for anyone, from the layperson to the opining expert. As such, the author's views are addressed to practitioners and individuals who must necessarily in their everyday endeavors present arguments supporting opinions to others before them.

From that perspective, the author proposes practical ways to apply the conceptual framework that is presented, together with illustrations of the concepts and suggestions on how to develop a well-defined and open analytical process that can lead to credible outcomes.

These concepts can be universally applied across many fields of endeavor, from executive decision making and professions to appraisal disciplines and many others, in order to solve everyday situations and problems.

As individuals who are the ultimate "triers" of fact in search of a truth, decision makers and stakeholders rely on opining individuals who offer credible opinions and arguments for their consideration and ultimate decision making.

In this framework, credibility becomes part of the journey to a truth.

In the next chapter, we will examine the elements, attributes, and surrounding factors that have an impact on credibility; we will propose an operational definition of credibility and will present tools that can be used to assess it in a variety of settings, from the appraisal disciplines to executive decision making.

And so, our journey begins.

The Solution

C REDIBILITY IS AN INFERENCE DRAWN by decision makers, resulting from an understanding of a well-defined process applied to a set of facts and circumstances under consideration.

 ## TOWARD A DEFINITION OF CREDIBILITY

Let us examine the implications of the above definition of *credibility*.

"Credibility is an inference . . ."

Credibility should be looked on as a state of mind resulting from the application of logical reasoning derived from factual knowledge or information.

This perspective implies that in order to set the basic premise of credibility, a logical conclusion drawn from factual knowledge is necessary.

Later on, you will see that this factual knowledge must be derived via the application of relevant analytical procedures to a given set of facts and circumstances to be set forth.

". . . drawn by decision makers,"

This part of the definition emphasizes the importance of the stakeholders or the decision makers as the ultimate purveyors of truth. It reminds us that credibility, in order to be an attribute of the work performed, must also be believed by the decision makers.

". . . resulting from an understanding of a well-defined process . . ."

To be credible, one must be able to clearly articulate the process that was used to conduct the analysis. Later on, I will introduce another underlying premise to this aspect of the definition of credibility, namely, that to be credible, opining individuals must "climb the Credibility Pyramid" and, while doing so, demonstrate an understanding of the conceptual framework defining credibility, in order to be able to proffer resulting credible opinions.

". . . applied to a set of facts and circumstances under consideration."

Once the process undertaken has been clearly defined, it must also be shown to be relevant to the matter at hand—that is, relevant to the facts and circumstances under consideration. The need for relevance is a key component of reaching credible results.

 ## THE ATTRIBUTES THAT MAKE YOU CREDIBLE

Now, with the above definition of *credibility* in mind, let me follow up with a framework that can be used to assess whether any given process is "credible" and continue with the development of the thesis of this book and its foundational approach to opined problem solving.

The credibility framework developed by the author consists of two aspects:

1. The credibility attributes that attach to the work product of an opining individual, which will be referred to as operational credibility attributes and discussed next.
2. The credibility attributes that attach to the opining individual, which will be referred to as personal credibility attributes. These include, for example, the education, training, and experience of the opining individual, to be discussed later on.

So, first let's discuss the credibility attributes that users can attach to the work product of an opining individual. Those attributes are referred as operational credibility attributes, to emphasize their closeness to the facts and circumstances that are under examination, as opposed to the personal credibility attributes, which will also influence the inferences drawn by a decision maker, but which may not necessarily have a direct relationship to the facts and circumstances of an engagement but will nevertheless be relevant to the overall decision-making process.

OPERATIONAL CREDIBILITY ATTRIBUTES

Credibility can be defined by the presence of nine operational attributes, applied to the various steps of an engagement:

1. Replication
2. Relevance
3. Reliability
4. Reasonable tests
5. Generally accepted methods and procedures
6. Transparency
7. Adequate disclosures
8. Nonadvocacy
9. Completeness

Replication

To be credible, your analytical work and any related developmental assumptions, conclusions, and summations must provide a path for others to follow, together with the means to replicate your work and obtain similar results. This approach to your foundational analysis should result in supportable conclusions that can be examined by anyone reviewing your work product.

Relevance

This refers to the specific relationship of your analytical nexus to a particular methodology or procedure forming a supportive and probative basis of the opinion to be offered. *Relevance* has also been defined as "Sufficiently tied to the facts of the case that it will aid the jury in resolving a factual dispute."[1]

Moreover, relevance requires that your foundational basis, in addition to being probative of your opined results, assist the stakeholder or the decision maker in resolving disputed fact issues.

For example, if your objective is to value a minority interest, reaching conclusions that cannot be attributed to a minority interest will cause your opinion to lack relevance and therefore stand on a flawed foundation, because such an analysis would not aid in determining the conclusion of the value of the subject minority interest, as no connection was established between the analysis made and the minority interest to be valued. Similarly, applying a discount rate derived from net cash flow to a net income–defined benefit stream would also be irrelevant.

If the information and the analysis that you present are not relevant to the facts and circumstances of the engagement, you will not be able to form a probative foundation, and thus, your work product may add nothing to the worth of your opinion. To make matters even worse, in fact, it may turn out to be speculative and prejudicial:

> We review the district court's decision to admit or exclude expert testimony for an abuse of discretion. See *Kumho Tire Co. v. Carmichael*, 526 U.S. 137, 152 (1999).
>
> A decision to exclude expert testimony is not an abuse of discretion unless it is "manifestly erroneous." See *McCullock v. H. B. Fuller Co.*, 61 F.3d 1038, 1042 (2d Cir. 1995). The district court's "gatekeeping" function in evaluating expert testimony requires that it look to Federal Rule of Evidence 401 to determine whether the testimony is relevant; i.e., whether it "ha[s] any tendency to make the existence of any fact that is of consequence to the determination of the action more probable or less probable than it would be without the evidence." See *Campbell ex rel Campbell v. Metro. Prop. & Cas. Ins. Co.*, 239 F.3d 179, 184 (2d Cir. 2001) (quoting Fed. R. Evid. 401).
>
> As the district court recognized, plaintiff's expert Dr. Frischberg was not qualified to make an assessment of the cause of the demise of the business. His expertise was limited to calculating the value of the business. In making his calculations, he assumed that a "campaign of disparagement" caused Fashion Boutique's sales to decline.
>
> However, as discussed above, no evidence of such a policy existed. See *Fashion Boutique III*, 75 F. Supp. 2d at 237–238. Moreover, Fashion Boutique presented only one customer who heard defamatory statements directly from Fendi salespersons during the first year of the sales decline. The other twenty or so incidents that occurred later can hardly be blamed as the cause of the falling sales. To permit Fashion Boutique to present evidence of the value of the entire business in the

absence of evidence of widespread dissemination would invite the jury to award damages based on speculation. See *Sunward Corp. v. Dun & Bradstreet, Inc.*, 811 F.2d 511, 521 (10th Cir. 1987). Therefore, we agree with the district court that Dr. Frischberg's testimony assumed a causal connection that plaintiff failed to prove.[2]

Reliability

Your opinion must be the product of reliable principles and methods.

The methods used must also be demonstrated to be properly applied. Reliability may involve reliance on sources established to be credible. These requirements ensure that the replication criteria can be met.

In addition, your methodology needs to be supported by a proper application. Namely, the methodology must be applied following the generally acceptable norms and conventions used by other experts under similar facts and circumstances.

For example, suppose that you present a statistical analysis of a particular data set. Let's assume that your selected statistical technique is generally accepted and used by other valuation practitioners under similar circumstances. If, however, your data points were selected using judgmental sampling, rather than random sampling, your sample size may lack a statistical foundation.

Therefore, your results cannot be duplicated, and while your statistical technique was generally accepted, a departure was made when the sample was selected without a proper sampling technique, thus lacking statistical foundation.

Improper application of procedural requirements of otherwise reliable methodologies is also a common error that can make an opinion flawed.

As is the case with these attributes, reliability is directly related to other attributes, such as relevancy and completeness. The reasoning is that if you included all of the relevant facts known or knowable as of the valuation date, the results that you concluded on can be consistently applied: Giving due consideration to the totality of the evidence before us, we find Mr. Davis' report to be more reliable than that of Mr. Kleeman. We agree with, and therefore accept, Mr. Davis' analysis. We do so for the following reasons:

First, Mr. Davis properly considered the relevant factors: (1) The relative size of the Trust's block of stock in relationship to the number of shares of stock outstanding, (2) the ownership of other blocks of stock, (3) current and historical trading volumes of shares of Applied Power stock, and

(4) recent company-specific events. Mr. Davis also reviewed general economic conditions and securities market trends and sentiment.

Second, in determining the size of the blockage discount to be applied, Mr. Davis tabulated information relating to eight 50,000-share-plus-trading days of Applied Power common stock in 1993, comparing the stock's closing price on each of those days with its previous day's closing price, and noted that the largest down tick trading day was 2.5 percent, whereas on one of the largest trading volume days there was an up tick of 1.5 percent. On the basis of this comparison, Mr. Davis concluded that only a modest blockage discount would be appropriate.[3]

It is interesting to note that in the following opinion, in discussing "reliability," the opinion also referenced another credibility attribute, that of "general acceptability," when it refers to the trial judge's determination as to whether the testimony given has a reliable basis in the knowledge and experience of the relevant discipline:[4]

Delaware Rules of Evidence 702 and 703 require a trial judge to act as a "gatekeeper" and to screen scientific, technical, or specialized opinion evidence in order to exclude from consideration such evidence as it finds to be unreliable as a matter of law. n.81 Cinerama's motion to strike the Klopfenstein testimony raises issues of relevance and reliability under Rules 702 n.82 and 703. n.83 Where, as here, the factual basis, data, principles, [and] methods of an expert or "their application" in connection with his opinion are called into question, "the trial judge must determine whether the testimony has a 'reliable basis in the knowledge and experience of [the relevant] discipline.'" n.84.

n.81 Daubert v. Merrell Dow Pharmaceuticals, Inc., 509 U.S. 579, 589, 113 S. Ct. 2786, 125 L. Ed. 2d 469. Accord M.G. Bancorporation, Inc. v. LeBeau, 737 A.2d at 522; Kumho Tire Co., Ltd. v. Carmichael, 526 U.S. 137, 147, 119 S. Ct. 1167, 143 L. Ed. 2d 238; General Electric Co. v. Joiner, 522 U.S. 136, 139 L. Ed. 2d 508, 118 S. Ct. 512 (1997).

n.82 Rule 702 provides: "If scientific, technical or other specialized knowledge will assist the trier of fact to understand the evidence or to determine a fact in issue, a witness qualified as an expert by knowledge, skill, experience, training or education may testify thereto in the form of an opinion or otherwise."

n.83 Rule 703 provides, in relevant part, that the "facts or data in the particular case on which an expert bases an opinion or inference" if "of a type reasonably relied upon by experts in the particular field in forming opinions or inferences upon the subject . . . need not be admissible in evidence."

n.84 Kumho Tire Co., Ltd. v. Carmichael, 526 U.S. at 147 (emphasis supplied), quoting Daubert v. Merrell Dow Pharmaceuticals, Inc., 509 U.S. at 592. Accord M.G. Bancorporation, Inc. v. LeBeau, 737 A.2d at 523.

Reasonableness

You should look for additional methodologies outside of your selected methods that justify your conclusions.

Reasonableness tests should be performed prior to the formulation of your opinion; they are part of your foundational analysis, leading up to and supporting your opinion. Reasonableness tests should embrace any alternative explanations, whether supportive or contradictory to the conclusions reached beforehand. The attribute of reasonableness also requires that any methodology employed be tempered with the application of informed judgment.

These reasonableness methodologies should provide confirmatory tests, separate and apart from the valuation opinion, and, in fact, these reasonableness tests need not be as generally accepted as the primary methodologies that were used as a foundation for your opinion.

Reasonabless procedures may also help to enhance the relevance and/or reliability of a particular conclusion:

> We are mindful that as a general rule only facts known at the valuation date are considered in determining the property's value. However, subsequent market activities may provide helpful comparable sales. See *Estate of Newhouse v. Commissioner*, 94 T.C. 193, 218 n.15 (1990). Here, we believe the three sales by the Trust within 3–1/2 months of decedent's death to be relevant and reasonably proximate to the valuation date. This 3-1/2-month period was, in our opinion, a reasonable period of time following the valuation date.[5]

In Chapter 7, I discuss reasonableness tests in more detail.

Generally Accepted Methods and Procedures (General Acceptability)

These are certain approaches, related methodologies, and procedures thereunder that have been peer reviewed and exposed to publication, which can be reasonably expected to be used by appraisers who are regularly conducting engagements under similar facts and circumstances.

Illustrating this concept, see the following opinion from a Tax Court Memorandum case: "We also find that the estate's experts' appraisals are more thorough and consistent with traditional appraisal methodologies for closely held companies like Kohler."[6] Similarly:

> For the reasons that follow, the court finds this methodology, with slight modifications, a reliable means of deriving MONY's fair value since such a metric is standard procedure in the financial community when valuing an insurance conglomerate consisting of diverse lines of business where no directly comparable companies or transactions exist.[7]

Situations can arise when generally accepted methodologies and/or procedures cannot be brought into the analytical process simply because of niche situations, or an unusual fact pattern, as noted in the following court case:

> As the second circuit has recognized, "thorny problems of admissibility arise when an expert seeks to base his opinion on novel or unorthodox techniques that have yet to stand the test of time to prove their validity." McCullock, 61 F 3d at 1042. As the three appraisers uniformly testified, what they do have in common is that despite 90 years of real estate appraisal experience among them, none has ever been confronted with an appraisal situation such as this. Thus each of the three appraisers was required to rely upon his own training, experience and education to devise a valuation methodology workable for this unparalleled appraisal task.

In such situations, opining individuals could supplement a newly devised methodology with the application of the credibility attributes as a means to overcome a lack of general acceptability.

Transparency

This refers to the inclusion and assessment of all known or knowable facts and circumstances, known to the opining individual, presented and considered without limitation. A transparent analytical process contains no firewalls, omissions, or inclusions of irrelevant facts preventing a user from having access to the information under consideration.

Adequate Disclosures

This refers to the requirement that the appraisal process must present information not only of all known facts and circumstances about the appraisal process undertaken, but it must also include sufficient, informative, and relevant disclosures to allow stakeholders in the appraisal process to understand the foundation of the appraiser's opinion.

Nonadvocacy

Nonadvocacy requires that you maintain a high level of objectivity in the formulation of your own independent expert opinion throughout all aspects of the process undertaken and, in particular, during the formulation and application of your informed professional judgment, as you construct the foundational analysis supporting your opinion.

Completeness

This requires that the data, assumptions, and explanations presented are described in enough detail to provide the stakeholder or the decision maker with an accurate depiction of the universe of transactions under consideration.

> Pump identified several additional flaws in Vollmar's analysis, as well. For example, Vollmar's report did not account for the historical financial performance of either the Technology or CLG, the future financial projected performance of the Technology or CLG, the industry in which the Technology would be used, the economic conditions at the time of valuation, market alternatives to the Technology, potential competitors of the Technology, risk factors, or investment considerations. (Id. 4494:13–4495:9.)
>
> Nor did Vollmar prepare any exhibits suggesting that his calculations or analysis incorporates these factors, each of which, in Pump's view, should be part of a valuation report. (Id. 4489:20–4491:25; 4495: 10–16.) In light of the need to take these factors into account, a valuation report for a simple business or a simple intangible asset would be at least twenty to thirty pages long, with five to ten exhibits, Pump stated. (Id. 4492:1–12.)
>
> Valuation of a new technology (such as the Cement-Lock Technology) is typically even more complex because of the lack of performance history. (Id.) Vollmar's valuation report was just two pages long, and the valuation analysis consisted of two paragraphs, comprising less than one full page. (Id. 4293:14–4494:3.)
>
> The report contained no exhibits that would illuminate the calculations. (Id. 4495: 10–13.)

As a result, Pump testified, Vollmar's analysis deviated sharply from what treatises require for valuation of an intangible asset: (1) detail and explanation consistent with the complexity of the asset; (2) supporting documentation to illuminate the logic and calculations; and (3) a discussion of the market in which the technology operates. (Id. 4496:4–4497:3.)

The business appraisal community also follows these guidelines. (Id. 4497:4–8.)[8]

The relationships among these attributes are depicted in Exhibit 2.1.

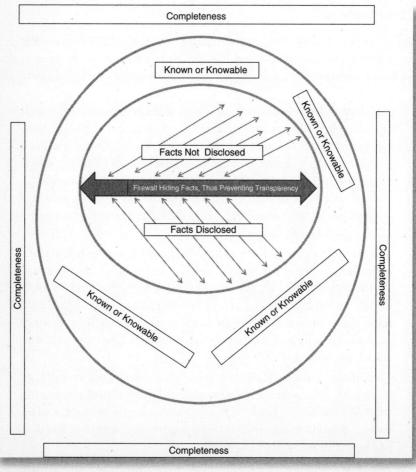

EXHIBIT 2.1 Completeness

As you can see, facts may be disclosed, and while adequate disclosures may be provided about those facts, firewalls may be introduced, perhaps unknowingly, which may preclude a user or a stakeholder from accessing or replicating those facts not disclosed. All of this points to the attribute of completeness, which may prevent this situation by requiring that all facts known or knowable are to be disclosed.

 ## PERSONAL CREDIBILITY ATTRIBUTES

The personal credibility attributes attach to the opining individual. Have you ever wondered why one opining individual may be believed more than his or her opposing counterpart?

The first factor for consideration is that these elements are brought to the engagement by the opining expert. Let's review those personal credibility attributes and how decision makers look on them:

- Education
- Training
- Knowledge
- Skill
- Experience
- Application of informed judgment
- Your personal and professional demeanor

These attributes are crucial before the opining individual is even hired, because they may determine the admissibility of the opining individual in most jurisdictions.

Because Messrs. Havemeyer, Hale and Dorchester were all offered as expert witnesses, at the outset the court must consider whether each of these individuals is qualified to testify as such. "The Federal Rules of Evidence permit opinion testimony by experts when the witness is 'qualified as an expert by knowledge, skill, experience, training or education' and 'if scientific, technical, or other specialized knowledge will assist the trier of fact to understand the evidence or to determine a fact in issue.'" *Zuchowicz v. United States*, 140 F.3d 381, 386 (2d Cir. 1998) (quoting Fed. R. Evid. 702). During the Daubert hearing, each of the proffered witnesses demonstrated that they have sufficient knowledge, skill, training and education to establish themselves as experts in terms of their "specialized knowledge" as to real estate appraisal. Indeed, with one slight exception which will be discussed below, in terms of their qualifications, none of the parties seriously challenged the ability of the three proffered real estate appraisers to testify in this case. Thus, in keeping with the Second Circuit's liberal interpretation of Rule 702, governing expert testimony, n4 because Havemeyer, Hale and Dorchester amply demonstrated through their respective curriculum vitae, and through their testimony, that they each have a "reliable basis in knowledge and experience," so that they are qualified to testify as experts on the issue of valuation methodology herein, the court finds that all three appraisers are qualified to testify as to that issue. See Kumho, 526 U.S. at, 119 S. Ct. at 1175.[9]

Note the reference in the above opinion to the two sources looked on by the court in determining the personal suitability of these three individuals, namely, their curriculum vitae and their testimony. The latter, one would expect; the former is increasingly overlooked by opining individuals.

An opining individual's curriculum vitae (CV) is normally required to be attached to the opined work product. This allows users of the work product to review that individual's credentials and the experience that he or she brings to the engagement in question. It is here, with the examination of the CV, that the importance of the personal credibility attributes comes to light.

An opining individual's CV should provide information in at least the following categories:

- Education
- Formal training in the field of expertise
- Professional licenses held
- Testimonial experience
- Professional affiliations and recognition awards
- Public speaking
- Teaching experience in the field of expertise

When it comes to these personal attributes, your CV should demonstrate a careful and well-thought-out approach to the topical areas in your continuing professional education, listed to readily complement and support your own knowledge base, thereby forming a foundation for those areas of expertise on which you will be opining.

It is common to review a CV that is lacking in any type of nexus or support in the areas of purported expertise. With a little thoughtful planning, this issue can be turned into a significant element toward your qualifications and credibility.

We will discuss informed judgment and your personal and professional demeanor in Chapter 9.

 ## GENERAL OBSERVATIONS ABOUT "CREDIBILITY"

"Credibility" also requires the existence of an overall nexus between the stated opinion and the above-referenced nine attributes and, in particular, relevance, reliability, completeness, and the reliable application of the methodologies used by the opining individual, in forming a basis for his or her stated opinion.

As part of the journey toward achieving credible results, the author has found the following general observations about credibility useful.

Credibility Is a Threshold

Once that threshold is crossed, adding more facts and additional analyses and issues can cause "paralysis by analysis" in the stakeholders' minds, resulting in diminishing returns for the opining individual. Successful opining practitioners tend to detect these thresholds and prepare their opinions accordingly.

Credibility Does Not Exist in a Vacuum

It is supported by collaborating elements—see the nine attributes discussed earlier.

Credibility Requires Consensus

When stakeholders begin to understand the relevance of your analysis to the issues before them, consensus begins to form among them, and your findings may begin to be perceived as credible.

Credibility Is the Result of Process

For the opining individual to be perceived as credible and thus worthy of belief, stakeholders need to understand the process he or she has undertaken. This process is defined as climbing the Credibility Pyramid.

In Chapters 3 and 4, I discuss the importance of knowing and understanding generally accepted practices in your own particular field of endeavor. As you will see, these generally accepted practices lay down a road map of the process that has gained consensus among practitioners. If you want to be credible, you must be able to use this road map.

Credibility Is Foundational and Dynamic in Nature

Where each layer of the foundation builds on and supports the stated opinion, as new facts become known or knowable, a credible analysis is able to assimilate them and incorporate them into any previously opined results. In addition, to be credible an opining individual may need to apply an interdisciplinary approach in the selected methodologies and procedures.

> Given the increasingly complex world in which we live, it is a fact of modern day life that many problems cannot be resolved without taking an interdisciplinary approach. Thus, the fact that both Hale and Dorchester relied upon other disciplines in devising their respective valuation models is of little consequence in terms of their qualifications to testify, particularly where, as here, each witness demonstrated his proficiency in the use of such disciplines in the context of real estate appraisal. Accordingly, as to the qualifications of the three appraisers, the court finds that each of them have the credentials, through education, training and experience, to offer their respective opinions as to the manner in which the subject property should be valued.[10]

To Be Credible, You Must Be Stakeholder Driven

To be credible, an opining individual should stand ready to understand the informational needs of the stakeholder or decision maker. This requires a consideration of the information needs of someone making a decision in a given capacity. For example, a bank trustee or a decision maker would have different needs, as opposed to a decision maker sitting as part of a judicial body. Consequently, any proffered opinion should be designed to help stakeholders and decision makers understand issues that are relevant to them. To do so, the opining individual must be stakeholder driven.

Moreover, risk of any sort is important to decision makers. Applying this simple commonsense approach, then, it would be useful to a decision maker if an opining individual identifies, as part of the analysis presented, the impact of any implicit attending risk(s), as defined in his or her own field of endeavor.

To Be Credible, You Should Also Be Thoughtful

A thoughtful opinion is centered on a reflective approach toward considering all available facts and alternative possibilities. Thoughtfulness, in this sense, refers to the proposition that to attain credibility, the stakeholder or the decision maker must be able to understand your efforts in objectively applying your informed judgment to the facts and circumstances at hand. You should also demonstrate an ability to identify with the information needs of your intended audience. Some opining individuals take the position that their goal should be to educate the stakeholder or the decision maker.

Certainly, educating your audience is a worthwhile undertaking and an important aspect of thoughtfulness.

The educational part of your analysis should be presented in a way that brings light where once darkness existed. By illuminating those facts and circumstances, you are also helping to identify critical aspects that must be understood by decision makers in resolving the matter at hand, and in this way you have identified the information requirements and the need-to-know elements of your analysis that will assist a decision maker.

Thoughtfulness in this context may also be demonstrated in the process that you used to climb the Credibility Pyramid. The following is an excerpt from a published opinion in a well-known valuation case (emphasis added): "We find that the estate's experts have *provided thoughtful, credible* valuations strongly supporting the value the estate reported on its tax return. . . . We accordingly give significant weight to their valuations."[11]

 ## CREDIBILITY IS NOT SYNONYMOUS WITH TRUTH

The search for truth has been a subject dwelled on by great thinkers from early civilizations to the present.

For our purpose, we work with the proposition that credibility is part of the path to a truth, and we take the position that only the decision makers and users of an opined work product can, or perhaps should, be the ultimate authority in this process, rather than the opining individuals.

The intent here is not to cast credibility in a relative fashion that can be shaped in any way or form to achieve a particular or perceived need. Instead, the purpose in separating credibility from truth is to propose the thesis that credibility must be part of any process pursued by opining individuals, whereas a truth must be sorted out and determined by decision makers charged with that duty, via the consideration of credible facts and analyses.

These assumptions lead to a key understanding, namely, that decision making and opining are two separate and distinct, yet, in most instances, complimentary endeavors. Decision makers and stakeholders, as individuals involved as the ultimate triers of fact in search of a truth, rely on opining individuals offering credible opinions and arguments to them for consideration and ultimate decision making.

In this framework, credibility becomes the journey to a truth, a vehicle that gets us to a truth.

A truth, by definition, exists independent of anyone, regardless of whether any one individual or group holds it as worthy of belief.

In this scenario, an opining individual passes on to a decision maker a credible opinion, based on an appropriate foundation, given a thorough analysis of the pertinent facts and circumstances.

On the other side, stakeholders run the final track of the relay race. They are the ultimate decision makers, as triers of any credibly opined result, and not the opining individuals.

I submit that credibility may point the way to a truth; however, credibility and truth are not the same thing and therefore should not be used interchangeably. The terms *credible, credibility*, or other variations of them are used in descriptive ways in many settings, as found in laws, regulations, professional standards, sets of criteria, and so on, yet an operational definition of credibility, with its own conceptual operational framework, has not been advanced.

A very simple but powerful definition of the term *credible* is found in the Uniform Standards of Professional Appraisal Practice, which define it as "something worthy of belief."

The power of these few words cannot be overlooked, yet the definition also points to some of the challenges facing opining individuals and decision makers alike. We will use this definition as a starting place to help us formulate an operational definition of credibility.

The phrase implies that a belief in something must exist and that such a belief, when adopted in the minds of individuals who hold that something as worthy, would cause it to be credible, and thereby credibility, as an attribute, would attach to it.

For example, one could easily refer to many instances in our everyday lives where particular beliefs are held as credible by groups of individuals, because these beliefs may serve some pragmatic point or purpose for them. However, another group may choose not to believe the same propositions and thus not hold them as truths.

DON'T CONFUSE OPINING WITH DECISION MAKING

Decision making and opining are two separate and distinct and, in most instances, complimentary endeavors.

Anyone opining before a decision maker should carefully consider separating the decision-making aspects of the endeavor from the opining process and the methodologies employed to proffer an opinion.

Where the work of the opining individual ends, the work of the stakeholder or the decision maker begins. Yet by understanding the stakeholders' decision-making process, an opining individual can be sure to introduce relevant information to the foundational process supporting the opinion.

The truth-seeking process is like a relay race, where one runner passes on the torch to the next runner, until the race is over—that is, until truth is determined. Using this analogy, an opining individual passes on to a decision maker a credible opinion, based on an appropriate foundation and grounded in a thorough analysis of the pertinent facts and circumstances.

Conversely, opining individuals should always keep in mind that the stakeholders or the decision makers run the final track of the relay race. Opining individuals must come to terms with the realization that their opinions are not the last word within any stated set of facts and circumstances, yet they are an important part of a process that should be construed to lead to the truth, regarding a set of facts and circumstances.

A given opinion, by and of itself, is not the ultimate result of a decision-making process; it is a part of the relay race. Opinions typically do not exist in a vacuum, and those that do exist in a vacuum tend to have very little utility.

Opining individuals are not decision makers; stakeholders are the ultimate decision makers. Keeping this perspective in mind may also help you:

- Stay within the parameters of your own field of expertise. Avoid becoming a "doctor of philosophy in the world's arts and sciences."
- Avoid giving legal advice in a legal or judicial setting—these are opinions that most individuals are not qualified to give, unless they are licensed to practice law in a given jurisdiction.

BEWARE OF BLACK BOX OPINIONS

Typically, the discipline of opining for the purpose of others relying on one's opinions is reserved to individuals who can stake positions as opining experts.

Unfortunately, individuals who stake positions as opining experts still ascribe to the proposition that an opinion given must be accepted as such, without providing any access to the foundational process that was used to derive it.

This type of opining can be characterized as a "black box opinion."

Many times, one may wonder whether a black box opinion originated with a well-meaning premise that all of the thought processes required to make a decision had already been undertaken during the formulation of the proffered opinion.

However, please consider that because any given opinion, in and of itself, is not the ultimate result of a decision-making process, it must be understood and be subject to assessment by the users, decision makers, and stakeholders in the overall process at hand.

CONCLUSION

And finally, if you still have any doubts, credibility can help establish reliance on the facts and the resulting analysis that are presented, so that stakeholders can then look to a proffered opinion to provide them with assurance that reliance on the opined results is warranted. Without credibility, there can be no reliance.

In addition, the credibility attributes discussed previously can be used to perform a qualitative review of the work product of another analyst (see Chapter 9).

These attributes can also serve to guide you as you perform your investigations and analytical processes and report on your findings.

So, with that thought in mind, now let's go to Chapter 3 and climb the Credibility Pyramid. Afterward, in Chapter 4, I will propose a definition of "informed judgment," as well as a definition of generally accepted practices and procedures, and explore how these concepts are also important components in the process of attaining credibility when opining.

NOTES

1. See *United States v. Downing*, 753 F.2d 1224, 1242 3d Cir. 1985.
2. *See *Fashion Boutique of Short Hills, Inc v. Fendi USA, Inc., et al.*, Citation No. 00-9094, 2nd Federal Circuit, 2002.
3. *Estate of Dorothy Foote., et al., Petitioner v. Commissioner of the Internal Revenue Service*, U.S. Tax Court, T.C. Memo 1999-37.
4. *Cede & Co v. Technicolor*, Delaware Supreme Court Citation, 2000, Lexis 283.
5. *Estate of Dorothy Foote., et al., Petitioner v. Commissioner of the Internal Revenue Service.*
6. See T.C. Memo. 2006-152, *UNITED STATES TAX COURT HERBERT V. KOHLER, JR., ET AL.,1 Petitioners v. COMMISSIONER OF INTERNAL REVENUE, Respondent*, Docket Nos. 4621-03, 4622-03, 4646-03, 4649-03. Filed July 25, 2006. Consolidated Brief, page 40.
7. See *Higfields Capital et al. v. Axa Financial. Court of Chancery of the State of Delaware In and For New Castle County*. Citation: 2007 Del. Ch. LEXIS 126. Decided August 17, 2007.
8. *Cement Lock et al., Plaintiffs, v. Gas Technology Institute, et al., Defendants*, U.S. District Court, Northern District of Illinois, Eastern Division, Case No. 05 C 0018.
9. See *Higfields Capital et al v. Axa Financial. Court of Chancery of the State of Delaware In and For New Castle County*. Citation: 2007 Del. Ch. LEXIS 126. Decided August 17, 2007.
10. See *The Cayuga Indian Nation of New York v. George Pataki*, U.S. District Court of New York. Citation: 83 F Supp 2d 318, 2000 U.S. LEXIS 761. Decided January 19, 2000.
11. See T.C. Memo. 2006-152 *United States Tax Court Herbert V. Kohler, Jr., et al.,1 Petitioners v. Commissioner of Internal Revenue*, Respondent Docket Nos. 4621-03, 4622-03, 4646-03, 4649-03. Filed July 25, 2006. Consolidated Brief, page 40.

CHAPTER THREE

The Credibility Pyramid and the Importance of a Well-Defined Analytical Process

A WELL-DEFINED ANALYTICAL PROCESS MAY WELL be the differentiating trait between an expert and a lay individual.

THE IMPORTANCE OF PROCESS

The above sentence is not intended to be dismissive of the utility that lay testimony may have in many different venues and occasions; it is simply intended to highlight the requirement underpinning the processes of opining individuals.

In doing so, I want to turn your attention to the importance of "process" as part of the credibility framework that we are developing.

So here is a definition of *process*:

> Process is a well-defined set of methods and procedures, subject to replication, applied with intellectual rigor and honesty, with the objective of seeking a resolution to a set of facts and circumstances, requiring a decision to be made.

The above definition may be very helpful when you are trying to explain to others what you did and how you did it in pursuit of your proffered opinion.

There are two important considerations to keep in mind:

1. The process must be clearly articulated.
2. The *scope* of the process must be identified and addressed throughout all phases of the analytical work undertaken.

Another proposition in this book is that *process*, as defined here, is part of the foundational framework that is required for one to be ultimately credible.

Why is this distinction of any consequence? Let's consider several possible scenarios. Assume that the truth of a matter is X.

Scenario 1: An incoherent and unsupported analysis of a set of facts is presented to you, as part of a decision-making committee.
   On that basis, the opining individual states that he or she believes that the opined result should be X.
Scenario 2: A conclusion is presented to you, as part of a decision-making committee, but without any analysis or consideration of any of the known attending facts.
   On that basis, the opining individual states that he or she believes that the opined result should be X.
Scenario 3: A coherent and well-supported analysis of a set of facts is presented to you, as part of a decision-making committee.
   On that basis, the opining individual states that he or she believes that the opined result should be X.

We must then consider the following two questions:

1. Could all three opining individuals be correct?
2. Are all three equally credible?

As to the first question, yes, all three opining individuals are obviously correct, because they present the truth of the matter at hand. However, are they all equally credible? A resounding *no*.

And therein lies the quagmire for decision makers. Whom should they believe? The answer *should* be that there is only one credible opining individual, scenario 3, the one with the well-defined process. Why?

Because a well-defined set of methods and procedures is subject to replication, is applied with intellectual rigor and honesty, and has the objective of seeking a resolution to this set of facts and circumstances, thus should pave the way for decision makers to fulfill their purpose and objectives: making the right decision in pursuit of a truth.

So now, let me give you a couple of examples on how to implement your well-defined process.

First, I will show you a sample of reporting language commonly used by valuation analysts in describing the valuation process they have undertaken.

THE VALUATION PROCESS

The valuation of an interest is, in essence, a prophecy about the future, based on a risk assessment of known or knowable relevant facts as of the valuation date that are likely to affect the realization of the identified benefit stream to a hypothetical buyer. A range of values, rather than an absolute value, best represents fair market value itself, inasmuch as the valuation conclusions derived by valuation analysts are the aggregate results of independent risk assessments, approximations, assumptions and limiting conditions, interpretations of known or knowable facts as of the valuation date, the application of common sense, and informed professional judgment and reasonableness, rather than mathematical certainty.

Factors considered by an appraiser during the valuation of a business enterprise are the pattern of historical performance and earnings, the company's competitive market position, the state of the industry, the experience and the quality of management, marketability, risk factors affecting the subject, and other relevant factors. These relevant factors are embraced in Internal Revenue Service Revenue Ruling 59–60. The purpose of this Revenue Ruling was to outline and review in general the valuation approaches, methods, and factors to be considered in valuing shares of the capital stock of closely held corporations for estate tax and gift tax purposes. The methods discussed therein will apply likewise to the valuation of corporate stocks on which market quotations either are unavailable or are of such scarcity that they do not reflect the fair market value. Generally accepted valuation practice requires the consideration of the eight factors listed in Revenue Ruling 59–60 as one of the basic requirements for reaching a credible valuation opinion of value. These eight factors are listed in Exhibit 3.1.

Following are reporting examples used by valuation analysts to define the scope of the valuation process.

EXHIBIT 3.1 Eight Factors

Revenue Ruling 59–60 Relevant Factors	Considered in This Appraisal Report In
1. The nature of the business and the history of the enterprise from its inception.	Section 3
2. The economic outlook in general and the condition and outlook of the industry in particular.	Section 2
3. The book value of the stock and the financial condition of the business.	Section 7.2 & Section 4
4. The earning capacity of the company.	Section 4 & Section 8.2
5. The dividend-paying capacity of the company.	Section 4.4
6. Whether the enterprise has goodwill or other intangible value.	Section 4.1
7. Sales of the stock and the size of the block of stock to be valued.	Section 7.1
8. The market price of stocks of corporations engaged in the same or a similar line of business having their stocks traded in a free and open market, either on an exchange or over the counter.	Section 7.6

Principal Sources of Information

The valuation analysis began with the receipt of certain information relating to the financial and operational performance of the company. This information included compiled financial statements and corporate income tax returns prepared by an independent CPA, unrelated to the appraiser. In addition, financial data and an analysis prepared by management were also provided. The company does not regularly prepare financial statements.

The members of management who provided significant input during the valuation process were Sonia L. Braga, president, and Josephine Baker, vice president.

(In this section you would identify the documents that you are relying on, such as tax returns, financial statements, opined reports from other individuals such as real estate and equipment appraisers, industry data and sources, and market data sources. You may also wish to indicate telephonic and/or personal interviews that provided input into your analytical process.)

Another example of a description of the process undertaken is found in the following discussion of a selected approaches and methods used in many valuation reports.

Income Approach

The income approach is based on the fundamental valuation principle that the value of a business is equal to the present worth of the future benefits of ownership. The factors driving this relationship can be expressed as follows. Value is determined by:

- How much economic benefit can be expected.
- Economic benefits captured by estimating a discount rate and the economic life of the benefit.
- Assessing risk factors, such as economic climate, competition, access to capital, and so on.

Under the income approach, two primary methodologies are used:

1. **Capitalized returns method.** This method, also commonly referred to as the *single period capitalization method*, is used when a company's earnings are stable, and long-term sustainable growth is expected to remain constant. This methodology is based on a determination of a particular level of income, based on earnings or cash flow, which is divided by a capitalization rate reflective of the investment risks associated with the subject interest. The term *income* does not necessarily refer to income in the accounting sense but to future benefits accruing to the interest being valued.
2. **Discounted future returns method.** This method, also commonly referred to as the *multiple period discounting method*, is used when future operations are expected to occur at fluctuating rates of growth until a sustainable rate of growth is reached. In applying this method, the valuation analyst estimates the future ownership benefits, based on some defined level of earnings or cash flow, and discounts them to a present value at an appropriate rate known as a discount rate. The discount rate should reflect the time value of money and the risks associated with ownership of the specific business or business interest that is the subject of the appraisal.

The single period capitalization and the multiple period discounting method both require the appraiser to make forecasts of future economic benefits. The multiple period discounting method requires estimates of future benefits over a specified period of time, usually 5 to 10 future years, until a sustainable level of future benefits is reached in the terminal period. Whereas, the single period capitalization method is based on a single period estimate of future economic benefits, such as the most recent year, and is a historical or forecasted weighted or simple average assumed to be the closest proxy for the forecasted future benefit stream. One of the challenges facing a valuation analyst using the income approach is accurately assessing the sustainable economic benefit that the subject company will be able to generate.

Section 5, *Weight to Be Accorded Various Factors*, of Revenue Ruling 59–60, states, "In general, the appraiser will accord primary consideration to earnings when valuing the stocks of companies which sell products or services to the public."

In accordance with the above requirement and in light of the relevant facts and circumstances of this engagement, the income approach was selected as one of the approaches that can yield a meaningful indication of value.

Standard and Premise of Value

In this section of your written report you should provide a clear understanding of the conceptual framework of the applicable standard of value. Note that later on in your analysis you may need to refer to these conceptual requirements to support your analytical procedures. We will explore this topic in further detail in Chapter 5.

THE CREDIBILITY PYRAMID

Climbing the Credibility Pyramid can be a process of working toward attaining credible results.

Process then becomes the differentiating element between the opining individual and anyone else who has cursory or general knowledge of the subject matter. For the opining individual to be perceived as credible and thus worthy of belief, stakeholders need to understand the process undertaken by that individual.

In this book, the process is defined as climbing the Credibility Pyramid. A failure to *effectively identify and communicate* the process undertaken, even if it is an otherwise well-defined process, can be problematic for stakeholders and can result in a loss of credibility for the opining individual.

As new facts become known or knowable, a credible analytical process is able to assimilate them and incorporate them into any previously opined results. This process makes it easier for stakeholders, decision makers, and users of opined results to hold a well-developed opinion as worthy of belief in the journey to the ultimate determination of the truth in a particular matter. Therefore, process becomes a fundamental tool, perhaps the most important tool, in an opining individual's approach toward the resolution of a set of circumstances, leading to a conclusion and ultimately a proffered opinion.

An opining individual should ground his or her opining process in a set of principles that is easily understood and subject to the assessment of another expert and/or stakeholder.

However, this is not an easy task, because most practicing opining individuals are inundated with myriad procedures and treatises, an ever-increasing body of knowledge, changing trends to be considered, as well as a continually growing and more complex set of professional standards. Where does it all end?

An expert should undertake the role of helping decision makers and stakeholders sort out the facts and circumstances that form the foundation for his or her conclusions and summations, ultimately resulting in the stated opinion. This foundational aspect forms the pyramid. In addition, this pyramid serves as a depiction of the process that an opining individual must "climb" in order to reach a credible opinion.

One of the central theses presented in this book is that to be credible, an opining individual must climb a Credibility Pyramid based on foundational elements. The foundational processes that make up the pyramid include planning, the opining individual's informed judgment, and the discipline's "body of generally accepted practices and procedures."

Those elements should be supportive of the opined results, in such a way that others can replicate the analysis that was presented, leading to the opinion proffered. Any given "opinion" can then be viewed as resting at the top of a pyramid, one that we build as an engagement progresses and, just as important, a pyramid that rests on the very foundation of the attributes that you, as an experienced opining expert, bring to an engagement.

Now, let me introduce you to a graphic representation of the Credibility Pyramid in Exhibit 3.2.

The analytical process should be based on the application of generally accepted practices and procedures typically used by other practitioners who face similar facts and circumstances. The implementation of a foundational process supporting your opinion is paramount to your attaining credibility.

The analytical process should be based on the application of generally accepted practices and procedures typically used by other practitioners who

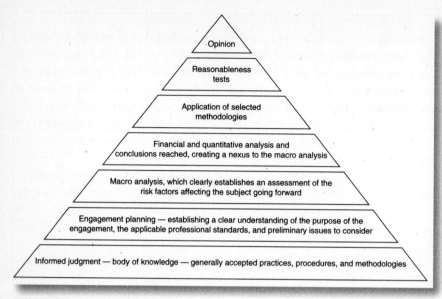

EXHIBIT 3.2 The Credibility Pyramid

face similar facts and circumstances. The implementation of a foundational process that supports your opinion is paramount to your attaining credibility. Why are these commonsense observations necessary? Because these precepts clearly begin to set the foundational framework that must be put together in order to be "credible."

 THREE PROBLEM-SOLVING PHASES

As you climb the Credibility Pyramid, three problem-solving phases should be dynamically considered.

The foundational part of most opining situations typically comes together via the congruence of three phases of a problem-solving process that need to be effectively coordinated during each foundational step; that is, at each level of the pyramid, these three phases may continue to manifest each time:

1. **The investigatory phase.** This is the planning phase of an engagement. Information is gathered. Effective engagement planning will help you avoid drifting into areas that lack relevance to the opinion.

2. **The analytical phase.** This phase may involve macro, as well as micro, analysis. Conclusions are reached from the application of methodologies.
3. **The reporting phase.** Conclusions are reached based on a synthesis of your findings at each step of the pyramid. The nexus of all of these conclusions leads you to the opinion. A report is prepared on the basis of related professional reporting standards applicable to the discipline. The reporting phase may conclude with either an oral or a written report; sometimes both may be used.

It is important to note that these phases may happen dynamically, simultaneously, and continuously; that is, as one phase progresses, a return to the previous phase may be required. For example, during the application of your selected methodologies, you may conclude that you need further data to be gathered and used in your analysis, and, in doing so, your conclusion may change; in other words, you may then conclude that the selected methodology is no longer appropriate, similarly, during the reporting phase. A common-sense observation is that you should always commence with the investigatory phase before proceeding to the analytical phase. Thorough detailed planning during the preliminary phases of each element of the pyramid can be very productive.

This concept also calls for the pyramid to become inverted as soon as we reach an opinion. Therefore, the opinion, once reached, now becomes inverted and supports the applied methodologies and the analytical work performed, even as additional facts and pieces of information may subsequently come to light, affecting the analytical work previously performed. Now, let us apply the Credibility Pyramid framework to a specific discipline, business valuations. See Exhibit 3.3.

During a typical valuation engagement, all parts of your written report should exhibit a connecting nexus. Then as you perform your analysis and reconcile your findings with generally accepted valuation methodologies, the resulting indications of value are incorporated into a valuation opinion.

Note that generally accepted valuation concepts also call for the foundational analysis to be incorporated into the reasoning used in the selection and application of the valuation approaches and the related methodologies that are used.

When applied to business valuations, the concept of the Credibility Pyramid proposes that your opinioned conclusions, during the developmental part of the engagement, be reached as you finish your foundational work. Your conclusions must also be grounded on the application of your informed judgment, which in turn results from your understanding of the facts and circumstances that you have identified in your economic, industry, and financial analyses of your subject.

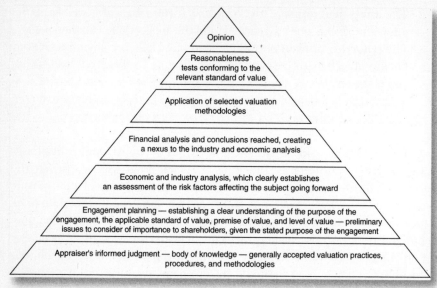

EXHIBIT 3.3 Business Valuations

We can also describe the business valuation process that a business valuator rendering an opinion of value needs to undertake (i.e., climbing the pyramid) in a simple flow chart. See Exhibit 3.4.

No matter how you may choose to refer to the process, either as a flow chart or as a pyramid, to be credible, you need to understand the nature of the conceptual attributes that make up the credibility framework.

Remember that the concept of "the Credibility Pyramid" proposes that your opinion, as well crafted as it may be and as otherwise credible as it may be, is not the truth of the matter at hand.

Your goal should be to render a credible opinion.

If you wish to explore the importance of process in further detail, I suggest that you turn to the United States Supreme Court Federal Rules of Evidence, which, in Article VII, "Opinions and Expert Testimony," promulgate Rule 701, "Opinion Testimony by Lay Witnesses"; Rule 702, "Testimony by Experts"; and Rule 703, "Bases of an Expert Testimony," where the very foundations for these principles are laid out.

For your ready reference, the actual text of Rules 701, 702, and 703 follows.

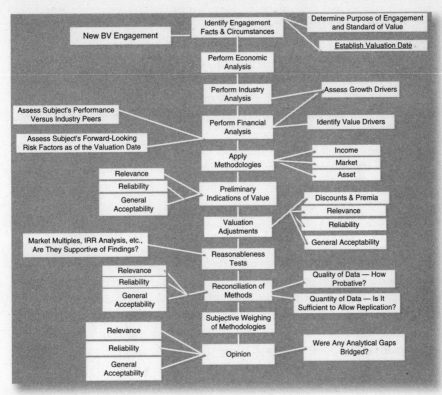

EXHIBIT 3.4 Climbing the Credibility Pyramid

Rule 701, "Opinion Testimony by Lay Witnesses"

If a witness is not testifying as an expert, testimony in the form of an opinion is limited to one that is

- Rationally based on the witness's perception;
- Helpful to clearly understanding the witness's testimony or to determining a fact in issue; and,
- Not based on scientific, technical, or other specialized knowledge within the scope of Rule 702.

Rule 702,"Testimony by Experts"

A witness who is qualified as an expert by knowledge, skill, experience, training, or education may testify in the form of an opinion or otherwise if:

- The expert's scientific, technical, or other specialized knowledge will help the trier of fact to understand the evidence or to determine a fact in an issue;
- The testimony is based on sufficient facts or data;
- The testimony is the product of reliable principles and methods; and,
- The expert has reliably applied the principles and methods to the facts of the case.

Rule 703, "Bases of an Expert's Opinion Testimony"

An expert may base an opinion on facts or data in a case that the expert has been made aware of or has personally observed. If experts in a particular field would reasonably rely on those kinds of facts or data in forming an opinion on the subject, they need not be admissible for the opinion to be admitted. But if the facts or the data would otherwise be inadmissible, the proponent of the opinion may disclose them to the jury only if their probative value in helping the jury evaluate the opinion substantially outweighs their prejudicial effect.

I find it useful to examine the proposition of these three rules from an educational perspective, within which, I submit, that "process" is expected to be an integral part of expert testimony, while lay witness testimony is expected to be based only on the perceptions of the lay individual, which, of course, may nevertheless be of interest to a trier of fact.

I submit that a display of intellectual rigor tacitly evident in the work product of an opining individual having a specialized understanding of the subject involved in the dispute typically points to a well-defined analytical process underpinning the foundational work supporting an opinion.

The above is not meant to imply that experts testify only by way of opinions but rather to explore the proposition that the pursuit of a truth resting within a given set of facts and/or circumstances may well be aided by the knowledge imparted from the application of an intellectually rigorous process.

This concept should not be new to most opining professionals, yet it is missed or dismissed more often than not in decision-making venues.

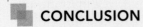 **CONCLUSION**

In the final analysis, if, as an opining individual, you wish to be found credible, then I submit that you need to have full knowledge of and command over the process undertaken in the formulation of your opinion.

The proposition that this book postulates is simple and generally supported by those who practice a discipline on more than an occasional basis.

Namely, that process must be present, be defined, and be subject to replication before an opining individual can be held as credible by a decision maker or a stakeholder.

In Chapter 4, we will take a look at the conceptual premises underlying generally accepted practices and informed judgment.

CHAPTER FOUR

Pyramids, Not Castles

C REDIBLE OPINIONS DON'T NEED TO be defensible. They can stand and survive the challenges of others on their own terms and foundations, without the need for any protective measures taken by those proffering them.

I view the process of climbing the Credibility Pyramid as an open and rigorous endeavor demonstrating the professional care undertaken by an opining individual that also points to the application of intellectual rigor to the effort involved.

Consequently, every time I hear the term *defensible* used in connection with *opining*, I pause and wonder whether the person I am listening to comprehends the inferences drawn by stakeholders and users of the opined work product when listening to the arguments and establishing the defensibility of a given position. It is difficult, if not impossible, to construct any type of foundational approach when you have to worry about being "defensible." The term *defensible opinion* may be found in many venues, from engineering to health care, accounting, law, and many others. You may run into some of the following variations:

- Defensible opinion of value.
- Defensible business valuations.

- How to make sure that your report is defensible.
- Ways to make your opinion defensible.
- How to make your arguments defensible.

There are many others. Now I would like you to think outside the box of an opining individual and paint in your mind's eye a picture of the term *defensible*. What do you see?

When I hear the word *defensible*, I see a picture of a medieval castle, surrounded by protective thick walls, accessed by a drawbridge, and surrounded by a moat, getting ready for a siege by invaders.

Well, if that image does not work for you, how about *Merriam-Webster*'s definition of the root term *defend*: " to maintain or support in the face of argument or hostile criticism . . . to attempt to prevent an opponent from scoring . . . to take action against attack or challenge."[1]

I think you would agree that the use of the term *defensible* conjures a negative aspect to opining that could easily be eliminated by use of the term *credible* instead.

Credible opinions don't need a castle surrounded by a moat, accessed by a drawbridge, in order to express or proffer a given point of view or perspective. Credible opinions are transparent and do not need layers of protective walls to keep others from seeing what is inside. When you are perceived as credible, there is no need to be defensible; the credibility attached to your work product will speak for itself.

WHY IS CREDIBILITY IMPORTANT?

Credibility is important because of one word: *reliance*. This is because stakeholders engaged in a decision-making process look to an opining individual to provide them with assurance that the work product presented can be reliably used.

If reliance is indeed the objective of an opining individual, then it is natural to assume that a stakeholder may be reluctant to rely on the work of an opining individual who is perceived as walking around in a suit of armor or whose opining and supporting methodology resides in, or requires protection behind, the thick walls of a castle.

Another way to look at this perspective is that it is difficult to embark on a journey in search of any given truth while you fear coming under siege. An opining individual should ground his or her opining process in a set of principles that is easily accessible and understood, without the presence of any firewalls or suits of amour, and subject to the assessment and replication of others.

Now we can start further development of the thesis of this book: its foundational approach to opined problem solving, based on the concept of credibility.

Before we proceed to discuss the role of general acceptability and informed judgment as important elements of the Credibility Pyramid, there are a few additional matters to consider.

Credibility Requires Execution

Over a period of years, I have observed otherwise competent and credible opining individuals "go down in flames" in their attempts to state an opinion. Their failure has been overwhelmingly due to an inability to execute conclusions and summations into a cogent finding, leading to an opined conclusion. Consider also that extensive analytical work may have been undertaken and, in my view, properly conducted, yet the opining individual could not reach a conclusion.

I refer to this mental shutdown and overload as "paralysis by analysis."

Opining individuals should keep in mind that stakeholders can also succumb to this "mental shutdown" when presented with an overload of information that virtually paralyses the senses and inhibits decision making.

Credibility Requires Inclusion of Alternative and/or Competing Views

As part of any analytical process that is presented, whenever appropriate, alternative explanations should be considered, evaluated, and fairly concluded on. A failure to consider alternative explanations to the proffered views, facts, and resulting conclusions can damage an otherwise credible position and may be perceived as an analytical process lacking in intellectual rigor and honesty.

Credibility Requires Consideration of Economic Realities

To be perceived as credible, your analytical process needs to step outside of any resulting conclusions and create a nexus to the outside world surrounding the facts and circumstances of your subject matter. For example, in the words of my friend Howard Lewis, if you are discussing a discount for lack of marketability, you should establish a nexus to the "market" that you are discounting from.

Credibility Requires a Nexus to the Underlying Data

To be perceived as credible, an opining individual should unequivocally demonstrate the probative value of the underlying data used in the analytical process to the opined results.

Credibility Requires Illustration

Some called it storytelling, while others like to refer to it as visualization of a journey to get to the opined conclusions. It certainly can be both.

I vividly recall an instance when I was tasked to provide expert testimony at trial as a valuation analyst. However, in a turn of the judicial proceedings, I was also requested to testify at an emergency hearing on the same case, calling for the appointment of a receiver.

One side of the case requested the appointment of a receiver on the grounds that the business had been mismanaged by a group of owners who were presently managing the business and now found themselves as respondents in these judicial proceedings.

The respondents argued, in turn, that management was trying to implement fundamental changes in the company's business model that were designed to deal with ongoing economic downturns and less-than-favorable industry trends that were affecting similarly situated businesses in the local economy.

My newly appointed role required me to offer a testimonial opinion to the court. As the hearing was scheduled on an emergency basis, my testimony was presented under a stipulation that it was based on the financial analysis, acquired knowledge of the company and its industry, that I had gathered as part of an ongoing valuation engagement related to other aspects of the case. The judge agreed to hear my testimony on this basis.

While waiting to be called to the stand, I challenged myself to find a way to state my opinion on this matter so that the judge could easily understand its intricate details.

I'm an avid boater, and an image came to me that this was an industry in the middle of a storm, a storm that could end up overtaking the company, just as a massive rogue wave could easily sink a vessel whose crew was engaged in a futile attempt to bail out the incoming seawater.

Here is the essence of how I concluded my testimony: "In conclusion, your honor, in my opinion, the present management's efforts are akin to an attempt to plug the hole in a sinking boat, rather than just adding another pump to bail out more water."

The judge accepted my opinion and ruled against the appointment of a receiver. To this day, I believe that the use of this analogy won that day in the courtroom.

 ## REASONABLE ASSURANCE

Now, let's turn to the concept of "reasonable assurance." Note that I am *not* referring to a "reasonableness test" or "reasonableness," which I will discuss later on.

Instead, I am referring to efforts undertaken as part of your internal in-house quality control procedures, designed to eliminate any speculative elements from interfering with your analytical process. In this way, we can define reasonable assurance as "safeguards inherent in your methodologies and procedures as you do your work, as well as any internal safeguards taken to mitigate any speculative issues while maintaining a high level of professional skepticism."

I am referring to reasonable assurance as a practice approach that should transcend every phase of your work, from the very beginning to the very end. Reasonable assurance can be a process that you implement to point out to users of your work product that internal safeguards are part of your opining process. So, as you progress through an engagement, you may continually ask yourself and your staff the following questions:

- Is the basis on which your opinion rests reasonable?
- Is the selected standard of value appropriate to the purpose of the engagement?
- Are the approaches and methodologies used the most appropriate to the level of value that you are reporting?
- Are there any limitations that you have to work around in order to reach a conclusion?
- Is there sufficient documentation in your work files to indicate the application of your informed professional judgment?
- Did you document the exercise of reasonable due care and due diligence commensurate with the requirements of the engagement?
- Is there satisfactory documented support in your files for your opinion?
- Were internal review procedures designed to cause a reexamination of the steps that you have taken during the engagement to eliminate any speculative aspects in your work and ultimate opinion before your opined work product is released?
- Have you documented a critical review of the magnitude of the valuation adjustments that you have made, in order to get to your opined number?

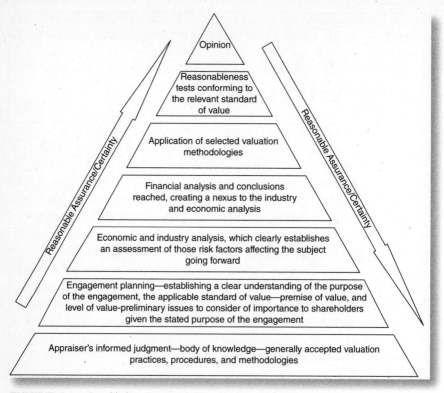

EXHIBIT 4.1 Credibility Pyramid, Plus Reasonable Assurance

A natural way to document the fulfillment of this criterion is to incorporate it into an internal quality control checklist (such as the one presented in Chapter 5).

With this concept in mind, we now proceed to modify and incorporate the precept of reasonable assurance into our Credibility Pyramid. See Exhibit 4.1.

Note that foundational process making up the pyramid includes planning, the opining individual's informed judgment, and the discipline's "body of generally accepted practices and procedures."

However, implementing these safeguards may not be an easy task, because most practicing opining individuals are already inundated with myriad checklists, procedures, treatises, articles, bodies of knowledge, the latest trends, and ever-increasing and more complex professional standards.

The approach to problem solving presented in this book rests on a key understanding, namely, that decision making and opining are two separate and distinct, yet, in most instances, complimentary endeavors. Furthermore, to be credible, opining individuals must "climb the Credibility Pyramid" and, while doing so, possess an understanding of the conceptual framework that defines credibility, in order to be able to proffer resulting credible opinions.

For example, during a typical valuation engagement, the economic, industry, and financial analyses performed should have a connecting nexus with one another, all of which are ultimately probative of the opined result. Similarly, as we climb the Credibility Pyramid, the generally accepted valuation methodologies that we execute would provide a reader with indications of value that would ultimately be incorporated into a valuation opinion. Note that generally accepted valuation concepts call for the foundational analysis performed during the economic, industry, and financial analyses to be incorporated into the reasoning used in the selection and application of the valuation approaches and the related methodologies that are used.

For illustration purposes, consider the following summary sections from a valuation report that I prepared:

Economic Section

The above referenced economic metrics point to volatile low-single-digit growth periods.

In conclusion, the valuation analyst's assessment of the aforementioned national and local economic factors, those most likely to affect the long-term operations of the Company, include:

- Improving long-term business investment and consumer spending.
- Improving consumer confidence.
- Maintaining stable consumer prices and low inflation trends of approximately 2 percent.
- Promoting low to moderate increases in employee average earnings levels and interest rates.
- Ensuring low to moderate increases in interest rate levels.
- Achieving an estimated long-term GDP growth rate of approximately 3 percent.

Industry Analysis

In conclusion, the Computer Systems Design & Integration Services industry sector looks like a period of tough belt tightening and low-single-digit growth, averaging approximately 3.2 percent, provided that the forecasted economic levels previously mentioned can be attained.

Financial Analysis

The valuation analyst concluded that the subject could be expected to continue operating at or above the industry performance averages; however, there is considerable risk that future earnings may deviate from the industry forecasts, due to volatile economic factors.

After concluding the economic, industry, and financial analyses sections of your report, you should now ask yourself the pertinent questions I presented to you earlier in "Reasonable Assurance." By providing answers to these questions during your analysis, you are in effect demonstrating to stakeholders and users of your work product the internal effort you have undertaken in the application of your intellectual rigor to assure yourself that your analytical work is void of speculative elements.

You should continue with this analytical approach as you climb each step of your Credibility Pyramid.

When applied to business valuations, the concept of the Credibility Pyramid proposes that your opinion of value, during the developmental part of the engagement, is reached as you conclude your foundational work, based on the application of your informed judgment, which in turn results from the application of your findings to the facts and circumstances that you have identified in your economic, industry, and financial analyses of your subject.

GENERALLY ACCEPTED PRACTICES

Generally accepted practices offer uniformity among practitioners, which in turn provides reliability of the attained results; consequently, they are important components of the perception of credibility.

A Body of Knowledge

The importance of a recognized body of knowledge, which we can refer to as generally accepted practices, is also critical to the process of establishing credibility. In this way, stakeholders can reasonably expect uniformity of practice among individuals who would opine before them. Most disciplines contain a body of knowledge that is followed by professionals actively engaged in each discipline. This expectation is important, because it differentiates the "professional" from the layperson, who has only cursory knowledge or experience in the subject matter under discussion.

As commonly defined, *generally accepted practices* refer to the approaches and related methodologies and procedures thereunder that have been peer reviewed and exposed to publication. I have found that most practitioners do tend to agree on the "how" aspects of their professional endeavors. Indeed, it is here where consensus tends to build among practitioners.

Before we go any further, though, let me expand on the above definition of *generally accepted methods and procedures*, which can apply universally to most professions and disciplines: Generally accepted appraisal practices in the United States are those approaches, related methodologies and procedures thereunder that have been peer reviewed and exposed to publication *and that can be reasonably expected to be used by other practitioners who are regularly conducting engagements under similar facts and circumstances.*

If we are willing to accept the above definition, then users of our work products can reasonably expect uniformity of practice among practitioners. This uniformity of practice among practitioners is the bedrock of credibility. In order to be credible, an opining individual must be well versed in the practices and procedures generally followed by individuals practicing in his or her field of endeavor. Opining individuals must possess the necessary education and training in their respective bodies of knowledge. They must be thoroughly familiar with the generally accepted practices and procedures prevailing within their disciplines. Those who are unfamiliar with the methodologies and procedures used by their peers to solve problems, under similar facts and circumstances, are likely to encounter a great deal of resistance from stakeholders and any users of their opined work products.

Consequently, if you are to consider yourself a member of a particular profession, then you need to remember that one of the defining characteristics of any profession is the recognition of a body of knowledge that must be mastered by individuals who practice such a profession. It is also important to note that the public expects those who practice a profession to be well versed in the prerequisite prescribed body of knowledge.

Nevertheless, there may be instances where opinions must be given, such as in niche situations or newly emerging fields of endeavor, where a body of generally accepted practices has not yet evolved or in instances where, during the development of your informed judgment, you may conclude that departures need to be taken, given your reasoned consideration of the attending facts and circumstances in your analysis. Then, in those instances, the burden should be on the opining individual to establish the reasoning for the departure.

I recommend the application of the "operational credibility attributes" as a proxy benchmark for general acceptability, discussed in Chapter 2.

Also, recall that in Chapter 2 I listed replication as one of the operational attributes of credibility, because replication can provide a path for others to follow. It is easier to believe in something that can be replicated; conversely, it is difficult to believe in something that lies within an expert's "black box," which users and stakeholders may not be able to evaluate. Thus, replication can be thought of as a subset of credibility, one that may not ensure the correctness of the results, but one that, at least, clearly sets a path that others can follow in the search for credible opined results.

So, as you go over your report, you should ask yourself whether you took any departures from generally accepted methodologies during the course of your analysis. If you had no choice but to depart from generally accepted methodology, then you must follow the applicable professional standards that deal with such departures.

Avoiding Misunderstandings

The following excerpt from a presentation at the 2011 AICPA National Conference on Current SEC and PCAOB Developments highlights some public misunderstandings that can arise, which could be easily avoided if the emphasis were placed on finding consensus among generally accepted practices, rather than presupposed differences in professional standards, as the following excerpt, in my opinion, erroneously implies. If you stop and consider that there is a trend for congruency among business valuation organizations, and that even without it, those professional standards contain more similarities than differences, and in most instances, share similar objectives.

> Valuation professionals stand apart from other significant contributors in the financial reporting process for another reason, their lack of a unified identity. We accountants, for example, have a clearly defined professional identity. At last count, valuation professionals in the US can choose among five business valuation credentials available from four different organizations, each with its own set of criteria for attainment, yet none of which is actually required to count oneself amongst the ranks of the profession. There are also non-credentialing organizations that seek to advance the interests of the valuation profession. While the multiplicity of credentials in the profession is not a problem

in and of itself, risks may exist. Risks created by the differences in valuation credentials that exist today range from the seemingly innocuous concerns of market confusion and an identity void for the profession to the more overt concerns of objectivity of the valuator and analytical inconsistency.

The fragmented nature of the profession creates an environment where expectation gaps can exist between valuators, management, and auditors, as well as standard setters and regulators. While much of this may be addressed during a particular engagement, this case-by-case approach has the potential to be an inefficient and costly solution to establish a baseline level of understanding of the analyses.

(For your reference, the complete presentation is available at www.sec .gov./news/speech/2011/spch120511pab.htm.)

General acceptability, replicability, and uniformity of consensus are common issues overlapping the boundaries and parameters of one or more disciplines or fields of endeavors. Yet as earlier proposed, credibility does not happen in a vacuum, but rather in a dynamic and, many times, interdisciplinary fashion. Indeed, the universe of solutions to any one particular issue or problem may relate to more than one discipline or field of endeavor.

Assessing General Acceptability in the Determination of Value

When assessing general acceptability in the determination of value, a business valuation practitioner may be guided by the following sources of generally accepted appraisal practices and procedures, which represent a compilation of overlapping disciplines and venues, from tax and fiscal compliance to judicial doctrines such as matrimonial and other judicial areas, as may be deemed appropriate, given the facts and circumstances under consideration and the application of that practitioner's informed judgment:

- Revenue Ruling 59–60
- Professional standards promulgated by accrediting organizations
- Uniform Standards of Professional Appraisal Practice (USPAP)
- Published treatises that have been generally embraced by valuation practitioners
- Judicial doctrines and relevant case law (always consult beforehand with legal counsel)

However, to be generally accepted, your analysis must rely on the same tools used by other experts in your field, when forming opinions or inferences under similar facts and circumstances. The reason being, that applying the same generally accepted methodologies to the same fact patterns should produce a reliable application of the methodology to the underlying facts, as well as allow for replication of the original results. Consequently, the concept of *reliability* is of great interest to a user of your work product.

Namely, users must be able to reasonably assume that reliance on your work product is justified, because your peers would have used similar methodologies under similar facts and circumstances and thus would have reached conclusions similar to yours.

GENERALLY ACCEPTED PRACTICES LEAD TO UNIFORMITY AND PROFESSIONAL CONSENSUS

This uniformity of practice among practitioners is at the bedrock of credibility. Uniformity does not mean that all opinions need to follow the same procedural development; rather, it refers to the underlying developmental process stipulating that opinions should be developed on a basis similar to the one reasonably relied on by other opining individuals, within the same field of expertise and, don't forget, *when dealing with the same set of facts and circumstances.*

Uniformity of practice also makes it possible for the results of a practitioner to be "replicated." In general terms, if practitioners within a given field follow prescribed practices, then it is possible for individuals who may be reviewing the work of a particular practitioner to replicate any proffered results.

In conclusion, credibility, as defined here, requires that any methodology employed be consistent with generally accepted practices and procedures and for the opined work product to exhibit a high degree of transparency and non-advocacy. This concept of *credibility* also requires the existence of an overall nexus between the stated opinion and the relevance, reliability, completeness, and reliable application of the methodologies relied on by the opining individual in forming a basis for his or her stated opinion.

Remember, all of these elements, when working together, should enhance the utility of any opinion and be directly measured by the level of credibility assigned by the respective users and stakeholders.

A user's ability to duplicate your results is directly related to the sufficiency of the data, assumptions, and explanations that you presented in your report.

ANALYTICAL GAPS

Another credibility quagmire faced by those who proffer opinions is the ever present analytical gap. Analytical gaps are great divides between a set of proffered facts and the resulting conclusions, which cause a reader to take a leap of faith, with no opportunity to duplicate any of the indicated results.[2]

Analytical gaps, an inability to replicate information, failure to follow established generally accepted practices and procedures, and failure to establish a nexus to the economic realities surrounding the facts and circumstances of an engagement are sure signs of opinions lacking in credibility, as illustrated in the following well-known court case.

> Generally speaking, however, several of Jachym's models—namely, his shared synergies approach and his sum-of-the-parts/actuarial appraisal analysis—are more credible, and therefore form the underlying basis for the court's determination of fair value in this case.
>
> Strikingly, despite the industry standard of using a sum-of-the-parts/actuarial appraisal methodology to value an insurance conglomerate as a going concern, and despite the reliance this court typically places on the merger price in an appraisal proceeding that arises from an arm's-length transaction, Shaked provided no testimony about MONY's value pursuant to these important models.
>
> Shaked's valuation not only suffers because of these analytical gaps, it is also markedly disparate from market price data for MONY's stock and other independent indicia of value. Because Shaked's conclusions substantially deviate from these objective barometers, it is appropriate to use Jachym's opinion as a baseline for the court to formulate its own independent judgment as to a fair value for MONY.[3]

Similarly, the development of methodologies outside the realm of generally accepted practices can also be problematic:

> Under either an analytical gap approach or review of Trevino's opinion against the Robinson factors, I conclude that his opinion is unreliable. Trevino's analysis of the 44-page and 77-page reports was subjective, his assumptions were unfounded, his opinion has not been subjected to peer review, and his technique has an unknown rate of error.[4] In addition, I note that Trevino's theory appears to have been developed for the litigation in this case. "Opinions formed solely for the purpose of testifying are more likely to be biased toward a particular result."[5]

Not only did Trevino fail to look at the data behind the numbers on the 44-page and 77-page reports, but he assumed that aging the accounts would not be necessary. He did not do any analysis to determine whether the zero entries in the reports were due to a lapse of coverage, improper billing, reduced coverage, or other insurance problems. Trevino's assumptions regarding contract and noncontract patients are unsupported by the evidence, and the failure to test those assumptions renders his report unreliable. Trevino did not "connect the data relied on and his . . . to show how that data is valid support for the opinion reached."[6] There is simply too great an analytical gap between the data and Trevino's testimony.[7] "Reliability may be demonstrated by the connection of the expert's theory to the underlying facts and data in the case."[8] Because, inter alia, Trevino did not examine any underlying data, his expert testimony was unreliable. Based on this analysis, we conclude that the trial court abused its discretion in admitting Trevino's expert opinion. Likewise, it constitutes no evidence to support the jury's damage award.

 ## INFORMED JUDGMENT

As proposed in this treatise, informed judgment is a state of mind developed as a result of the application of a rigorous analytical process, intended to assist a user in sorting out, prioritizing, and concluding on relevant facts and circumstances.

The application of thoughtfully applied informed judgment may be the most critical aspect in crossing the credibility threshold mentioned in Chapter 2.

It is during the planning phase where the application of informed judgment commences. During this phase, your process should be grounded in a consideration and an inclusion of all known facts and circumstances (the good, the bad, and the ugly ones) as part of a defined process, which continually considers and evaluates all possible alternative explanations and reasons. Therefore, the planning phase can be extremely important.

During the planning phase, an opining individual should make every possible attempt to communicate with the stakeholders. In some settings, this may not be feasible, but, whenever possible, a request to do so should be attempted. These individuals take the position that opinions are based simply on the views or perspectives of people rendering the opinions, without offering any other ways that a stakeholder or a user of their opined results can review or assess what is being proffered.

These individuals feel that the very essence of opining is a self-contained process that happens inside the black boxes inside their heads (recall the discussion on black box opinion in Chapter 2). Stakeholders and decision makers in today's world tend to resist and indeed reject those views.

It is difficult, if not impossible, to conceive of a qualitative problem-solving approach without this encompassing the need to apply informed judgment.

For a historical perspective, opining individuals may wish to be guided by three types of venues wherein judicial analysis has reviewed the application of informed judgment. These venues are

- Eighth Amendment issues
- Judicial review of administrative decisions made by governmental agencies
- The Business Judgment Rule affecting corporate decision making by boards of directors

A review of this history points to several attributes worthy of consideration by an opining individual:

- Informed judgment should be based on the presence of *objective factors.*
- Informed judgment should involve a high level of thoroughness being evident in its consideration, which I like to refer to as the *application of intellectual rigor.*
- The validity of its *reasoning.*
- Its *consistency with existing pronouncements.*
- *Nonadvocacy, the need for intellectual honesty and objectivity.*

For example:

No static "test" can exist by which courts determine whether conditions of confinement are cruel and unusual, for the Eighth Amendment "must draw its meaning from the evolving standards of decency that mark the progress of a maturing society." *Trop* v. *Dulles,* 356 U. S. 86, 101 (1958) (plurality opinion). The Court has held, however, that "Eighth Amendment judgments should neither be nor appear to be merely the subjective views" of judges. *Rummel* v. *Estelle,* 445 U. S. 263, 275 (1980). To be sure, "the Constitution contemplates that in the end [a court's] own judgment will be brought to bear on the question of the acceptability" of a given punishment. *Coker* v. *Georgia,* supra, at 597 (plurality opinion); *Gregg* v. *Georgia,* supra, at 182 (joint opinion). But such "judgment[s] should be informed by objective factors to the maximum possible extent."[9]

In another venue dealing with administrative rulings by governmental agencies, we find the following observation regarding the application of informed judgment ruled by the U.S. Supreme Court:

We consider that the rulings, interpretations and opinions of the Administrator under this Act, while not controlling upon the courts by reason of their authority, do constitute a body of experience and informed judgment to which courts and litigants may properly resort for guidance. The weight of such a judgment in a particular case will depend upon the thoroughness evident in its consideration, the validity of its reasoning, its consistency with earlier and later pronouncements, and all those factors which give it power to persuade, if lacking power to control.[10]

In the following ruling by the Delaware Supreme Court, in referring to the business judgment, a measure of nonbias and nonadvocacy is described as underpinning elements in the application of business judgment:

> Given the foregoing principles, we turn to the standards by which director action is to be measured. In *Pogostin v. Rice*, Del.Supr., 480 A.2d 619 (1984), we held that the business judgment rule, including the standards by which director conduct is judged, is applicable in the context of a takeover. *Id.* at 627. The business judgment rule is a "presumption that in making a business decision the directors of a corporation acted on an informed basis, in good faith and in the honest belief that the action taken was in the best interests of the company." *Aronson v. Lewis*, Del.Supr., 473 A.2d 805, 812 (1984) (citations omitted). A hallmark of the business judgment rule is that a court will not substitute its judgment for that of the board if the latter's decision can be "attributed to any rational business purpose." *Sinclair Oil Corp. v. Levien*, Del.Supr., 280 A.2d 717, 720 (1971).

> When a board addresses a pending takeover bid it has an obligation to determine whether the offer is in the best interests of the corporation and its shareholders. In that respect a board's duty is no different from any other responsibility it shoulders, and its decisions should be no less entitled to the respect they otherwise would be accorded in the realm of business judgment. See also *Johnson v. Trueblood*, 629 F.2d 287, 292–293 (3d Cir.1980). There are, however, certain caveats to a proper exercise of this function. Because of the omnipresent specter that a board may be acting primarily in its own interests, rather than those of the corporation and its shareholders, there is an enhanced duty which calls for judicial examination at the threshold before the protections of the business judgment rule may be conferred.[11]

In summary, the development of informed judgment brings together an opining individual's training and experiences in that field of expertise and the facts and circumstances encountered in solving a problem.

For our purpose, informed judgment can be operationally defined as

- The aggregate result(s) of assessments, conclusions, summations, and approximations resulting from the process undertaken by an opining individual.
- Premised on the application of intellectual rigor, common sense, and reasonableness, consistent with generally accepted practices.
- In light of differing interpretations of known or knowable facts.
- Applied to the problem-solving process undertaken.
- Using generally accepted practices, applied on a basis of objectivity, reasoning, and nonadvocacy.

Consequently, there will be differences of opinion over any one set of facts and circumstances, inasmuch as the derived conclusions are the results of aggregate risk assessments, approximations, assumptions and limiting conditions, differing interpretations of known or knowable facts, the application of common sense, informed professional judgment, and reasonableness, rather than mathematical certainty.

In this way, informed judgment can be applied in a reasoned objective fashion and indeed differentiated from the application of purely subjective methodologies.

As earlier discussed, the application of informed judgment should rest on an analytical process that can be subject to replication by others and, at the same time, also include some immeasurable but reasoned intangible element.

In our final analysis, any given opinion rests at the top of a pyramid, one that we build as an engagement progresses and, just as important, a pyramid that rests on the very foundation of those attributes that you, as an experienced opining expert, bring to an engagement.

 ## CONCLUSION

This chapter explored several new perspectives that are supportive of the proposition that credibility is an inference drawn by decision makers, resulting from an understanding of a process applied to a set of facts and circumstances under consideration, namely:

- Credible opinions are preferable to defensible opinions.
- General acceptability is defined in terms of similarly situated facts and circumstances.

▪ Informed judgment was defined in a way that unequivocally sets it apart from the application of raw subjectivity and unsupported assertions.

Chapter 5 discusses climbing the Credibility Pyramid.

 ## NOTES

1. Sourced from www.merriam-webster.com/dictionary/defend.
2. See *Highfields Capital Ltd., et al., v. AXA Financial, Inc. In the Court of Chancery of the State of Delaware In and For New Castle County.* Citation: 2007 Del. Ch. LEXIS 126. Decided August 17, 2007.
3. See *Highfields Capital Ltd, et al., v. AXA Financial, Inc. In the Court of Chancery of the State of Delaware In and For New Castle County.* Citation: 2007 Del. Ch. LEXIS 126. Decided August 17, 2007.
4. See *Robinson*, 923 S.W.2d at 557 (listing factors for determining the reliability of expert testimony).
5. Id. at 559.
6. See *Whirlpool*, 298 S.W.3d at 642.
7. See *Gammill*, 972 S.W.2d at 726.
8. See *TXI Transp.* Co., 306 S.W.3d at 239.
9. *RHODES, GOVERNOR OF OHIO, ET AL. v. CHAPMAN ET AL.* No. 80-332. Supreme Court of the United States. 452 U.S. 337 (1981).
10. See *SKIDMORE ET AL. v. SWIFT & CO.,* Supreme Court of United States No. 12. 323 U.S. 134 (1944). Decided December 4, 1944. Certiorari to the Circuit Court of Appeals for the Fifth Circuit.
11. See *Unocal Corporation, a Delaware corporation, Defendant Below, Appellant, v. MESA PETROLEUM CO., a Delaware corporation, Mesa Asset Co., a Delaware corporation, Mesa Eastern, Inc., a Delaware corporation and Mesa Partners II, a Texas partnership, Plaintiffs Below, Appellees.* Supreme Court of Delaware. 493 A.2d 946 (1985).

Climbing the Credibility Pyramid

C REDIBILITY IS AN INFERENCE DRAWN by decision makers, resulting from the application of an analytical process to a set of facts and circumstances under analysis.

 ## THE IMPORTANCE OF REVENUE RULING 59–60

Revenue Ruling 59–60 is generally accepted as a treatise of the factors to be considered in order to reach a credible opinion of value. As you might recall from Chapter 3, Exhibit 3.1 listed the eight factors generally regarded by valuation analysts as key elements to be considered.

As a valuation analyst, you must be conversant with these factors, and your valuation analysis must consider all of these eight factors as part of the process of climbing your own Credibility Pyramid.

For reporting and report-reviewing purposes, it is useful to list where in your report each of these factors was considered.

One of these factors requires consideration of the nature of the business, and the history of the enterprise from its inception is one of the requirements necessary to achieve a credible valuation.

Specifically, Revenue Ruling 59–60 further defines this requirement as follows:

> The history of a corporate enterprise will show its past stability or instability, its growth or lack of growth, the diversity or lack of diversity of its operations, and other facts needed to form an opinion of the degree of risk involved in the business. For an enterprise, which changed its form of organization but carried on the same or closely similar operations of its predecessor, the history of the former enterprise should be considered. The detail to be considered should increase with approach to the required date of appraisal, since recent events are of greatest help in predicting the future; but a study of gross and net income, and of dividends covering a long prior period, is highly desirable.
>
> The history to be studied should include, but need not be limited to, the nature of the business, its products or services, its operating and investment assets, capital structure, plant facilities, sales records and management, all of which should be considered as of the date of the appraisal, with due regard for recent significant changes. Events of the past that are unlikely to recur in the future should be discounted, since value has a close relation to future expectancy.[1]

Consequently, your credibility may be damaged if you fail to establish that you attained an understanding of your subject's operations, which is required for the proper determination of value to be undertaken. Indeed, professional due care supports the proposition that this guidance applies universally across most disciplines. Yet as simple and commonsense as this may sound, in actual practice one is likely to come across an opining work product that fails to meet this very basic guideline for the determination of value.

The following two comments from a trier of fact, on the same case, help illustrate this very basic requirement.

Note the contrast the court makes between the two opining experts: one expert who failed to attain a level of understanding of the subject's operations, as required by the purpose of the engagement, versus the two opposing experts who were able to establish crossing that credibility threshold (emphasis added).

> Dr. Hakala's background research on Kohler was limited. He met with Kohler management just once, for about 2-1/2 hours. He did obtain financial information from the company including both the operations plan and management plan, however, and considered industry information.

Moreover, we are convinced from his report and trial testimony that Dr. Hakala did not understand Kohler's business. He spent only 2-1/2 hours meeting with management. He decided the expense structure in the company's projections was wrong and decided to invent his own for his income approach analysis. He did not discuss his fabricated expense structure with management to test whether it was realistic.

After carefully reviewing and considering all of the evidence, we continue to find Dr. Hakala's conclusions to be incredible. We therefore give no weight to respondent's expert's conclusions. Respondent has therefore not met his burden of proof.

We now briefly describe the reports and valuation conclusions of petitioners' experts, Mr. Schweihs and Mr. Grabowski, each of whom we find thoughtful and credible. We *give significant weight to their reports, which lend further* support to our conclusions.

Mr. Schweihs had periodically performed valuations of Kohler stock in the several years before the valuation date and is very familiar with the company.

Mr. Grabowski spent 3-1/2 days at the company and interviewed 12 employees, spending considerable time with 6 of them, including Herbert (the President and Chairman of the Board) and Natalie (the General Counsel). Mr. Grabowski also reviewed numerous documents and considered general economic conditions and the industries in which Kohler

You must apply the necessary engagement resources toward the fulfillment of this commonsense requirement of knowing your subject, as part of your journey toward achieving credibility.

You should plan on spending a significant amount of time conducting site visits, management interviews, and meetings with various levels of management to make sure that you acquire an in-depth operational understanding of the facts and circumstances underpinning any given engagement.

IDENTIFICATION OF KEY PRE-ENGAGEMENT PARAMETERS

Early on, you should define the engagement parameters and confirm them with the prospective client prior to formulating your engagement agreement. For a valuation engagement, key parameters that should be identified are

* The valuation date.
* A clear and unequivocal definition of the interest to be valued.
* The purpose of the engagement.
* The standard of value to be used.
* The type of information to be provided.
* The expected due date of the report.
* The expected date of commencement.
* The contact individuals for the engagement.
* The type of report to be prepared.
* The intended users of the report to be prepared.

The interest to be valued should be carefully defined, to include all of the ownership characteristics of the interest, and should be stated in the same way that it will be stated in the opinion to be proffered. Avoid summary and incomplete descriptions, such as "a 55 percent equity interest in the class B shares." Instead, such an interest should be described in detail; for example, *The interest to be valued comprises 300 Class "B" Common Share, representing a fifty-five percent (55%) Interest, on a not freely marketable control basis, in the $30.00 par value Class "B" Common voting stock, authorized, issued and outstanding, Valued as a single block.*

The purpose of an engagement should be defined as narrowly as possible, keeping in mind that the stated purpose may drive the approach and the methodologies that are to be ultimately used, in addition to potentially affecting the scope of the engagement.

In addition to a detailed discussion of the appropriate standard of value for the engagement, you should also make sure that the client's legal counsel collaborates and, whenever appropriate, provides and/or confirms the appropriate the standard of value, as well as the premise of the value to be used. A sober discussion of these issues at the very outset will prevent unwelcome results later on.

The types or classes of documents to be provided should also be discussed during the planning phase. Such a discussion may point to possible areas where limitations on the scope of your analytical process could affect the opinion.

The contact individuals for the engagement should have enough knowledge, training, or experience to intelligently understand and proceed to procure the documents and the information requested.

The type of report should be determined. Beware of situations where a single report is to be used for the valuation of more than one subject interest. This can be very confusing and should be avoided.

Looking to the stated purpose of the engagement, you should inquire about the classes of intended users. Always remember to include such intended users as the Internal Revenue Service in all tax-related valuations.

 ## PLANNING TO ACQUIRE KNOWLEDGE ABOUT THE SUBJECT

Now let us turn to some specific guidance that may help you climb your own pyramid in the planning phases of an engagement. Whenever possible, these recommendations are stated in a principles-based fashion, so that they can be implemented in other fields of endeavor, in addition to the determination of value.

The planning phase is extremely critical. During the planning phase, the opining individual should make every possible attempt to communicate with the stakeholders. In some settings, this may not be feasible, but a request to do so should be made. During the planning phase, the opining individual should start to visualize the risks and obstacles that will need to be overcome, how these elements will affect the analysis to be undertaken, the scope of the data-gathering process that will be required, and the chance that any potential scope limitations could ultimately narrow the usefulness of the opined results.

The opining individual's knowledge and experience with the subject matter play an important role in the planning phase. It is during the planning phase where the application of informed judgment commences. There are several points that you will need to explore in detail:

- The history of the company
- Where the company is headed
- Management's vision to guide the company
- The strategic steps under consideration to execute that vision

Notice that the perspective you must assume is both historical and prospective (that is, forward looking) in nature. Therefore, in order to reach a solid understanding of these matters, you should perform some preliminary research on the industry before you proceed with your analytical process. Some practitioners like to do this even before interviewing any members of the management team. Choose a style that suits your personal preferences.

However, regardless of how you choose to proceed, you should try to identify current events at the national, state, and local levels that affect your subject. Do you possess any specific knowledge or training that may be helpful in identifying risks, rewards, and uncertainties potentially affecting your subject?

Take an inquisitive, while at the same time skeptical, approach to your quest for knowledge during the planning phase. This attitude should help you maintain a higher level of intellectual rigor. You should inquire of management *why* events presented to you unfolded as discussed. You should attempt to identify the facts and the circumstances that led up to those events. Once you have reached an adequate level of understanding, then you should ask for supporting documents to assist you in further comprehending the subject matter.

Below, you will find a simple 10-point checklist (see Exhibit 5.1) that I developed and use when interviewing members of management. I use it in a casual and conversational way. Note that several of these topics may be discussed later as value drivers that either enhance or detract from any derived valuation proposition in pursuit of the proffered opinion of value.

In addition, these topics may help you identify risk factors to consider. See Exhibit 5.1.

EXHIBIT 5.1   Value Drivers and Risk Factors Questionnaire

Topic No.	Area of Inquiry	Present	Not Present	Relevant (Y/N)	Possible Impact on This Valuation
1	Assessing a company's strengths and operations				Low asset base, with high levels of earnings, may imply the presence of intangibles as major value drivers. Inquire about the company's customer-generation ability, the nature of the workforce in place, and how customer lists are compiled, maintained, and used. Inquire about patents, trade names, or special licenses. Also inquire about the presence of technical or business know-how, secret processes, etc., that enhance the cash flow–generating capacities of the firm.

Topic No.	Area of Inquiry	Present	Not Present	Relevant (Y/N)	Possible Impact on This Valuation
2	Are there any concentrations in terms of customers, suppliers, or product lines?				The quality of a company's earnings-generation capacity is affected by any of these concentrations. That does not mean that the presence of concentrations is a "bad thing"; instead, it may point to a higher-risk-based enterprise than one that is more diversified.
3	Are there effective internal controls in place and a culture of honest financial reporting?				Management should be able to demonstrate that it has historically monitored internal financial performance and pursued decision making on the basis and strength of its financial reporting. Furthermore, the presence of effective internal controls should be a vehicle in the execution of management's strategic objectives and in measuring how effectively the company's vision has been pursued.
4	What are the levels of management?				Typically, management depth is lacking in many closely held business concerns. Therefore, a closely held business concern that has demonstrated an ability to transfer the necessary operational knowledge and practices to other members of the team in a logical and well-thought-out fashion is typically less risky than one that has not done so.

(Continued)

EXHIBIT 5.1 (*Continued*)

Topic No.	Area of Inquiry	Present	Not Present	Relevant (Y/N)	Possible Impact on This Valuation
5	What is the company's track record of access to capital?				A demonstrated ability to gain access to external sources of capital may help lower risk.
6	Identify and, if possible, quantify the presence of favorable contractual relationships.				The quality of any material favorable to contractual relationships should be analyzed to determine the forward-looking expectations and continuing impact on profitability.
7	Inquire about the company's legal history, customer complaints, and regulatory compliance.				A continuing history of litigation, contractual breaches, customer complaints, and regulatory issues may be indicative of "negative goodwill" and related risk factors. Analyze the company's history regarding returns and allowances and warranty expenses.
8	Inquire about the effect of technological trends on the company.				Has the company maintained a policy that is supportive of its anticipated technological demands? Inquire as to how capital needs are determined and financed.
9	How does the company deal with its human resources?				Have the various levels of management and employees been supportive of the corporate goals? Does the company encourage in-house staff promotions, training, and incentive programs?
10	What is the company's strategic vision?				Has the management team been able to effectively execute the stated strategic vision? Has it clearly communicated its strategic vision it to others?

As part of the intellectual rigor that you exercise, you should explore alternative scenarios and try to look for the responses to these areas of inquiry on the subject going forward. I would encourage you to ask as many follow-up questions as you may feel are necessary, as you search for a thorough understanding of the nature, history, and outlook of your subject.

 ## GENERAL PLANNING CONSIDERATIONS

Once you have acquired a basic level of knowledge about your subject, you are now ready to move on to the planning phase of an engagement, which should include the following three steps:

1. Preparation of an engagement agreement.
2. Identification of relevant documents and information to be requested.
3. Obtaining a representation memo.

Preparation of an Engagement Agreement

Your engagement memo represents a contractual agreement between you and your client. Therefore, whatever form of document you decide to adopt for this purpose, you should consult with legal counsel beforehand. The information that follows is presented only for educational purposes and should not be referenced without the aid and interpretation of your legal counsel.

Your engagement agreement should be tailored to your type of practice and clientele. Do not adopt any language or terms that you do not fully understand. There are several reasons for this:

- You need to be able to explain the terms and conditions expressed in your agreement to your clients.
- If you are ever called to testify or become involved in any form of legal proceeding, your engagement agreement may come under close scrutiny.
- As your practice changes, you will need to make changes to accommodate the trends in your own practice.
- Changes in professional standards and/or related regulations may dictate changes to your engagement agreements.
- Different types of engagements may call for dramatically different agreements. One size does not fit all, that is, different professional standards may apply or different terms and conditions may apply, calling for a different agreement.

Keeping in mind the previous comments, following are some key areas that you should consider in the drafting of your engagement agreements. In addition, a sample engagement agreement is presented in this book's Appendix to illustrate the application of these concepts only from an educational perspective. Please consult with your legal counsel before adopting any of the provisions illustrated here.

Some of the key areas to consider in your engagement agreements are:

■ Objective, purpose, and valuation date
■ Definitions of the work product that is to be delivered
■ Commencement and completion
■ Definition of specific interest and level of value to be valued
■ Standard and premise of value
■ Fee schedule, payment terms, and conditions
■ Limiting conditions and assumptions of the agreement
■ Standards of practice and distribution of the valuation report
■ Conflicts of interest
■ Work papers and confidentiality
■ Client responsibilities
■ Fraud and internal controls
■ Reproduction of the valuation report
■ Services and costs not of this engagement and not included in the fee estimate
■ Settlement of disputes
■ Indemnification
■ Site visits
■ Privacy policy
■ Identification of the engagement team
■ Entire agreement
■ Time is of the essence: acknowledgment and time for acceptance

Identification of Relevant Documents and Information to Be Requested

As you might recall from Chapter 3, I identified three problem-solving phases to be dynamically considered:

1. **The investigatory phase.** This is the planning phase of an engagement. Information is gathered. Effective engagement planning will help you avoid drifting into areas that lack relevancy to the opinion.

2. **The analytical phase.** This phase may involve macro, as well as micro, analysis. Conclusions are reached from the application of methodologies.
3. **The reporting phase.** Conclusions are reached based on a synthesis of your findings at each step of the pyramid. The nexus of all of these conclusions leads you to the opinion.

As you begin climbing the Credibility Pyramid, your investigatory phase will need to be considered. You should take notice of the fact that in addition to documents that you will need, you should also consider making informational inquiries. To illustrate this point, I have included an information request that I sent to a client in connection with a recent engagement. Note the number of questions that I prepared specifically for this engagement. This case involved the determination of economic damages; however, as you can see from the questions presented, there were several valuation issues that had to be dealt with.

You should take the time to ask for specific documents and information that you will need to perform an engagement and resist the temptation to send your client a boilerplate document request.

You should also keep in mind that the responses to your document request may help point the way to changes in your assumptions about the engagement, as well as to possible limitations in the scope of your engagement.

Therefore, you should carefully monitor these responses, so that you can take the appropriate course of actions early on in the engagement. You should maintain a record indicating who provided the responses and the dates received.

Remember, this investigatory phase opens up the doors to your analytical phase and commences the application of your intellectual rigor, all necessary steps to earn the credibility that you want stakeholders and potential users to ultimately attribute to your opined work product. The following sample document request is intended to show you the application of these concepts universally across different types of valuation and valuation-related engagements.

Document Request Sample

> To: Purchaser of XYZ Aircraft
> Re: Determination of Economic Damages Engagement
> From: Mr. Analyst
> Name of Management Representative Providing Responses:

(Continued)

All items require a response. Indicate "N/A" for items not available or not applicable to your company.

Please provide in PDF format.

Where necessary, feel free to use the attached supplemental sheet provided at the end.

On receipt of your responses, we may request additional information.

General

Items Requested	Yes/ No	Received On	Pending	N/A
1. Please provide a narrative describing your background, with particular attention to any aspects relevant to this case.				
2. Please provide your responses to the attached questions in Addendum 1. Feel free to fully describe all matters affecting each question.				
3. What is the key selling feature of the XYZ serial number 123456 (XYZ Aircraft)?				
4. How is pricing determined for the sale of a new XYZ Aircraft? For new aircraft, are prices discounted?				
5. To what degree do competitors' prices affect the marketplace where the XYZ Aircraft is sold?				
6. Describe a typical purchaser of an XYZ Aircraft.				

Next, list XYZ Aircraft's major competitors and indicate with a checkmark, to the best of your knowledge, whether XYZ Aircraft has a greater or lesser comparative market share than the listed competing aircrafts.

Competition

Aircraft	Model Description	Comparative Market Share Greater/Lesser	Manufacturer
1.			
2.			

Aircraft	Model Description	Comparative Market Share Greater/Lesser	Manufacturer
3.			
4.			

Also, at the time of purchase, identify any factors to be considered by a prospective purchaser of an XYZ Aircraft.

List any known XYZ Aircraft's strengths versus its competitors'. List any known XYZ Aircraft's weaknesses versus its competitors'.

Facilities and Flight Operations

	Yes/ No	Received On	Pending	N/A
1. Describe your local market regarding the availability of qualified personnel to service and maintain an XYZ Aircraft.				
2. Was the XYZ Aircraft a part of any contract, flight club, owner's club, or any other arrangement designed to reduce the costs of owning an airplane?				
3. Describe how many hours the XYZ Aircraft was flown, according to its official flight logs.				
4. Describe the original purpose for your acquisition of the XYZ Aircraft.				
5. Please provide a copy of any existing lease prior to the sale of the XYZ Aircraft. Were there any lease termination costs? Were current rents on these leases at or near market rates?				
6. List each hangar location where the XYZ Aircraft was kept (location or address).				
7. Were there any excessive or extraordinary overhead costs associated with the operations or maintenance of these facilities?				
8. Did you own any hangar buildings or facilities that were used to store or maintain the XYZ Aircraft?				

(Continued)

	Yes/ No	Received On	Pending	N/A
9. What is the overall condition of any avionics, landing gear, or any other aircraft elements, including the air frame, unaffected by the alleged matters in this complaint? Was there any inefficient or obsolete avionics equipment? Was the XYZ Aircraft in need of major repairs or landing gear or engine overhauls?				

Aircraft Dealers

	Yes/ No	Received On	Pending	N/A
1. List the names of any factory-authorized aircraft dealers providing sales, maintenance, and support for the XYZ Aircraft in your general vicinity?				
2. List the names of any other aircraft dealers supporting the XYZ Aircraft in your general vicinity:				
A.				
B.				
C.				
D.				

Subsequent Events

	Yes/ No	Received On	Pending	N/A
1. Please provide a narrative describing any events taking place after your sale of the XYZ Aircraft that, if known prior to the sale, by either you or the buyer, could have affected the terms and conditions of the sale.				

Addendum 1

Please provide a typed response for each of the following questions or statements:

- Please state the name of the buyer of the XYZ Aircraft.
- Are you related to the buyer directly or indirectly in any way?
- Was the buyer a dealer or a private party?
- Was the buyer experienced in this type of aircraft?
- How did you come in contact with the buyer?
- What were the selling price and the terms of the sale?
- Did you receive any other consideration, in any form, in addition to the selling price?
- If so, please describe any other consideration received.
- Did you make any repairs in order to make the XYZ Aircraft air worthy, or was the XYZ Aircraft sold "as is"?
- If the XYZ Aircraft was sold "as is," describe the scope of any repairs that the buyer was expected to undertake in order to make the XYZ Aircraft air worthy.
- How many hours of flight time had been logged in at the time of the sale?
- Other than the alleged air-worthiness issues listed in the complaint, was the XYZ aircraft due for any major overhauls or repairs at the time of the sale?
- Other than the alleged air-worthiness issues listed in the complaint, during the term of ownership was the XYZ Aircraft damaged in any way?
- If so, please describe the nature of any damage to the XYZ Aircraft.
- During the term of ownership, was the XYZ Aircraft involved in any accidents or incidents?
- Describe the advertising media that you used to expose the XYZ Aircraft to the marketplace.
- Geographically, please describe the markets where you offered the XYZ Aircraft for sale.
- Describe any other means that you used to expose the XYZ Aircraft to the marketplace.
- How did you establish the asking price that was used in your attempts to sell the XYZ Aircraft?
- How many offers did you receive?

(Continued)

- Chronologically, approximately, when were these offers received?
- Describe the terms of each offer received from prospective qualified buyers.
- Was the offer accepted the highest offer received?
- If the offer accepted was not the highest received, please describe the factors you considered in accepting it.
- How long was the XYZ Aircraft exposed to the marketplace before the sale?
- To the best of your knowledge, were you aware of any issues known in the marketplace of potential buyers affecting the selling prices of XYZ Aircrafts offered for sale as of the sale date?

Supplemental Response

Make as many copies as necessary. Give the name of the management representative providing the responses. Indicate when any attached documents are included to supplement your response.

Re: Document Request 2

Supplemental Response Sheet #:

Date:

Category:

Question Number:

Supplemental Response:

I suggest that every time that you send an information request to a client, you include a privacy policy disclosure, which is intended to inform your client on how you plan to use this information. As there may be legal considerations involved, you should consult with qualified legal counsel to assist you. The following is an example of a privacy policy that I typically use.

Sample Privacy Policy: Exhibit Analysts, LLC

Valuation analysts, like all providers of financial services, are now required by law to inform their clients of their policies regarding the privacy of client information. In addition, we have been and continue to be bound by professional standards of confidentiality that are even more stringent than those required by law.

Types of Nonpublic Personal Information We Collect—We collect nonpublic personal information about you that is provided to us by you or obtained by us from third parties with your authorization.

Parties to Whom We Disclose Information—For current and former clients, we do not disclose any nonpublic personal information obtained in the course of our practice, except as required or permitted by law. Permitted disclosures include, for instance, providing information to our employees and, in limited situations, to unrelated third parties who need to know that information to assist us in providing services to you. In all such situations, we stress the confidential nature of information being shared.

Protecting the Confidentiality and Security of Current and Former Clients' Information—We retain records relating to professional services that we provide so that we are better able to assist you with your professional needs and, in some cases, to comply with professional guidelines. In order to guard your nonpublic personal information, we maintain physical, electronic, and procedural safeguards that comply with our professional standards.

Obtaining a Representation Memo

An engagement representation memo may be used at the conclusion of an engagement in order to memorialize relevant facts and circumstances that affect the opined results.

While it may appear to be redundant with respect to an engagement agreement, the demarcation between these two documents is that an engagement agreement is prepared prospectively, namely, at the inception of an engagement, when many matters are not known at the time of its execution. Conversely, a representation memo is prepared on conclusion of an engagement, at a time when all matters have been satisfactorily resolved.

Consequently, new issues may have arisen that now need to be addressed prior to the conclusion of an engagement. Following are some of the provisions that you may wish to include in a calculation of value engagement:

The client represents to the analysts that to the best of its knowledge and belief—

1. Management has made available to the analysts all information requested and relevant to the calculation of value engagement.

2. Management is not aware of any information provided to the analysts found to be inaccurate, incomplete, negligently prepared, or misleading.

3. The income tax returns furnished to the analysts for the years 20XX through 20XX are complete and exact copies of the returns filed with the Internal Revenue Service, and no amendments have been filed or were contemplated to be filed with the Internal Revenue Service, as of the date of this memorandum.

4. Any commitments or contingent liabilities, including those arising from litigation, claims, and/or assessments, are disclosed in the information provided to the analysts.

5. The company does not have any (a) employment contracts with salaried employees, (b) stock option plans, or (c) stock redemption agreements with shareholders.

6. Except for the prospective sale of the company, management is not currently negotiating the acquisition of new business interests or the disposition of existing segments or product lines.

7. You agree that the analysts have communicated with you regarding all matters relevant to this engagement, and that no additional relevant facts or circumstances regarding this engagement have become known to you prior to the conclusion of this engagement.

8. You understand that the calculation of value report will be subject to assumptions and limiting conditions, which are included as an integral part of the calculation of value report.

9. As of the date of this memorandum, it is management's intention that the company will continue to operate as a going concern, that the character of its present business will remain intact, and that the company will be competently managed and maintained by financially sound owners.

10. You acknowledge your understanding that this engagement cannot be relied on to disclose errors, fraud, or other illegal acts that may exist or that may have occurred.

11. The client and the analysts agree that no conflict(s) of interest existed or developed during the course of this engagement to prevent the analysts from rendering an unbiased calculation of value.

12. You agree to carefully read and review the calculation of value report prepared by the analysts, and unless you notify the analysts within three days after receipt of it, the analysts will properly conclude that the information about the company presented therein is accurate and complete.

THE IMPORTANCE OF THE STANDARD OF VALUE AS YOU CLIMB THE PYRAMID

During the planning phase, a sober look at the requirements of the engagement should lead to an in-depth consideration of the particular issues attendant to the standard of value on which the opinion of value is to be framed within. In fact, an effective way of referring to standards of value is to think of a standard of value as a "framework," a framework that determines the "four corners" of your analysis. A valuation analyst should careful study the requirements of a particular standard of value and assess the resulting effect on the scope of a valuation engagement. The improper application of a standard of value may cause great harm to an unaware valuation analyst. Before accepting an engagement, a valuation analyst must have a thorough understanding of the requirements of a particular standard of value. The selected standard of value should be indicated on the engagement memorandum to be prepared. This is a great planning engagement tool that can also help establish the exercise of due reasonable care by a valuation analyst during the formative phase of an engagement.

Fair Market Value

For illustration purposes, consider the following report language:

> The standard of value required by this engagement is Fair Market Value, applied to the Common Stock of Consolidated Components, Inc., a Florida "S" Corporation.
>
> "Fair Market Value" is defined, under Revenue Ruling 59–60 and related United States Treasury Regulations, as the price at which property would change hands between a hypothetical willing buyer and a hypothetical willing seller when the former is not under any compulsion to buy and the latter is not under any compulsion to sell, with both parties having reasonable knowledge and access to all relevant facts.
>
> For this valuation, the definition of fair market value also includes the following assumptions: (i) the hypothetical parties are prudent but without synergistic or other strategic benefits, (ii) the hypothetical parties are able as well as willing to enter into a transaction, (iii) the interest appraised is assumed to be sold for cash or its equivalent on the Valuation Date in a hypothetical arm's length transaction between a nonspecific hypothetical willing buyer and a nonspecific hypothetical willing seller, (iv) the Appraiser acting as a surrogate for

both hypothetical buyer and seller in determining the independent opinion of value.

The hypothetical buyer under the fair market standard is considered a financial and not a strategic buyer. Likewise, the hypothetical seller is considered to be offering the interest for sale without any indicia of compulsion, or special interests or concerns.

Therefore, the definition of fair market value excludes buyers and sellers who because of other activities brings some value added benefits, which would enhance the company being valued, and/or the buyer's other activities, e.g., being acquired by other companies in the same or similar industry. This also excludes buyers or sellers who are already shareholders, related or controlled by an entity who might be willing to acquire the interest at a higher or lower price due to considerations not typical of the motivation of the arms-length financial buyer/seller transaction. The estimate of fair market value relied on a "value in use," or going concern premise. This premise assumes that the Company is an ongoing business enterprise, with no plans to liquidate, with management operating in a rational way with a goal of maximizing shareholder value over an indefinite life of the enterprise.

And more important, the credibility of an opinion will diminish if the above considerations are not correctly implemented throughout the analysis performed.

"Matrimonial" Standard of Value

Now let's look at matrimonial engagements. Consider the following matrimonial report language that is defining the matrimonial standard of value to use. Note how the definition of *fair market value* has been expanded to include its application to material issues considered later on during the valuation analysis conducted for a matrimonial dissolution engagement, where the state law requires the application of fair market value as the standard of value:

> The standard of value required by this engagement is Fair Market Value, applied to the valuation of the Subject interest in Information Systems Designs, Inc., a Florida "S" Corporation, *for marital dissolution purposes.*
>
> "Fair Market Value" is defined under Revenue Ruling 59–60 and related United States Treasury Regulations as the price at which property would change hands between a hypothetical willing buyer and a

hypothetical willing seller when the former is not under any compulsion to buy and the latter is not under any compulsion to sell, with both parties having reasonable knowledge and access to all relevant facts.

For non-marital purposes, the definition of fair market value also includes the following assumptions: (i) the hypothetical parties are prudent but without synergistic or other strategic benefits, (ii) the hypothetical parties are able as well as willing to enter into a transaction, (iii) the interest appraised is assumed to be sold for cash or its equivalent on the Valuation Date in a hypothetical arm's length transaction between a nonspecific hypothetical willing buyer and a nonspecific hypothetical willing seller, (iv) the Appraiser acting as a surrogate for both hypothetical buyer and seller in determining the independent opinion of value. The hypothetical buyer under the fair market standard is considered a financial and not a strategic buyer. Therefore, the definition of fair market value excludes the buyer who because of other activities brings some value added benefits, which would enhance the company being valued, and/or the buyer's other activities, e.g., being acquired by other companies in the same or similar industry. This also excludes buyers who are already a shareholder or a related or controlled entity who might be willing to acquire the interest at a higher or lower price due to considerations not typical of the motivation of the arms-length financial buyer. The estimate of fair market value relied on a "value in use," or going concern premise. This premise assumes that the Company is an ongoing business enterprise, with no plans to liquidate, with management operating in a rational way with a goal of maximizing shareholder value over an indefinite life of the enterprise.

For purposes of this matrimonial appraisal assignment, the following definitions will be used:

- **Goodwill** is the advantage or benefit a business has beyond the value of its property and capital, which is property that attaches to it and is dependent on an existing business entity.
- **Enterprise goodwill** is the value of earnings or cash flow directly attributable to the enterprise's characteristics or attributes, separate and distinct from the presence and reputation of the owner spouse. Enterprise goodwill, sometimes referred to as *practice or business goodwill*, is a function of the continued expectation of earnings from repeat customers who will patronize the business, as opposed to the owner spouse.

■ **Personal goodwill** is the value of earnings or cash flow directly attributable to the owner spouse's reputation, personal characteristics, or attributes. Personal goodwill, sometimes referred to as *professional goodwill*, is a function of the earnings from repeat business that will patronize the owner spouse, as opposed to the business.

The purpose of this assignment, as stated in Section 1.3 above, requires consideration of the following five factors in the valuation analysis:

1. The valuation of the subject interest will also be considered within the context of a "value in exchange." According to authors Jay Fishman, Shannon Pratt, and William Morrison,[2]
    ■ To the extent that the conclusion of value estimates depends on the continued efforts of one party, that portion of the value is excluded and viewed as separate property or not as property at all.
    ■ States following a value in exchange premise reject the inclusion of intangible value reliant on an individual for several reasons, including the viewpoint that postmarital efforts are necessary to realize the value and also that the property allegedly created is not capable of being separated from the person.

On this basis, enterprise goodwill will be part of the valuation of the subject interest. Conversely, any amounts that are considered to depend on the continued future efforts of the owner spouse and attributable to that spouse will be determined to be personal goodwill, and thus excluded from the determination of fair market value under this appraisal assignment.

2. For a determination of the factors considered probative by the appraiser in the determination of personal and enterprise (business) goodwill, see Section 6.1.1.
3. The value of any noncompete covenants will be assumed not to be a marital asset, because such agreements were considered to relate to a postmarital activity.
4. No built-in gains tax liabilities will be calculated since:
    a. No court disposition of the subject interest is assumed.
    b. As a result, no tax liability is imminent.
5. For purposes of this valuation, goodwill and any intangible assets not separately identified (that is, workforce in place, customer lists, intellectual property, and so on) were considered together and indistinguishable from goodwill itself.

In many jurisdictions, the statutory standard of value called for in matrimonial engagements may be fair market value. Yet there are many instances where case rulings point to results that may not necessarily align with the fair market value framework. Therefore, in order to preserve the credibility of your proffered results, you will need to adapt your reporting language to the appropriate jurisdictional requirements

Fair Value

Many valuation analysts tend of think of the standard of value as something that is mentioned at the outset of the valuation analysis and, hopefully, in the opinion language. This lack of awareness of the importance of conducting your valuation analysis within the framework of the selected standard of value typically leads to numerous analytical gaps.

For example, many valuation analysts erroneously think of statutory "fair value" as differing from fair market value, in that fair value does not encompass valuation adjustments, such as the discounts for lack of marketability and the discount for lack of control.

This is a serious misconception. Fair value, depending on the facts and circumstances of a given engagement, may or may not consider synergistic elements; statutory fair value involves consideration of such concepts as "overall fairness," involving elements of procedural and absolute fairness. These concepts are material elements to be considered by a valuation analyst and a failure to properly consider them will erode the foundational aspects of a given proffered opinion.

As an illustration, I have found that when dealing with statutory fair value as a standard of value, a useful precept to keep in mind is to continually ask the question: Is the result fair to the oppressed party, the remaining parties, and the entity in its ability to continue as a going concern if the opined amount were to be adopted and implemented?

 SELF-ASSESSMENT TOOLS

In assessing the credibility of an opinion, your work product should be measured in terms of its adequacy, appropriateness, and reasonableness, developed within the context of generally accepted practices, normally relied on by others in your own field of endeavor, as of the date of your report.

There are simple tools that can help you assess your own credibility. For example, I developed the following report-writing checklist as a simple credibility self-assessment tool. See Exhibit 5.2.

EXHIBIT 5.2　Report Writing Qualitative Checklist for Any Discipline

Credibility Element	Present in Your Report (Y/N)	Identify Opportunities for Improvement	Corrective Actions Taken
Does the report tell a story, commencing with a well-defined table of contents? Does the report take the reader on a journey leading to the opined conclusion, following a well-defined road map?			
Does the report allow the reader to visualize the process pursued, thus keeping the reader engaged?			
Is the report concise and void of generalizations?			
Does the report establish that the principles and methods used were relevant to the facts and circumstances under consideration?			
Is it clearly stated that the principles and methods used were reliably applied in the derivation of your opinion?			
Is the information presented in the report sufficient to allow duplication of the analysis presented?			
Is the report supported with logical reasoning? Were all assertions and estimates considered and concluded on?			
Does the report consider information, facts, and circumstances that other practitioners would consider under similar circumstances?			
Does the report account for alternative explanations and assumptions?			
Does the report pick and choose among purported facts to justify the appraiser's opinion of value?			

Now, let's apply the concepts in Exhibit 5.2 to the determination of value, and the result is a qualitative checklist I developed and use in practice, depicted in Exhibit 5.3.

EXHIBIT 5.3 Business Valuation Qualitative Case Review Checklist

Engagement _____

Valuation Date _____

Review Criteria	Findings (Pass/Fail)	Comments	Corrective Actions Taken
Does the sufficiency of the data, related assumptions, and explanations offered in the appraisal report allow duplication of the results presented?			
If sufficient data, assumptions, and explanations were provided, do they support the opinion of value?		Identify any sections you found insufficient.	
What is your assessment regarding the general acceptability of appraisal methods used?		Are the methodologies reliably applied?	
Is the financial analysis of the company (including comparisons to its industry peers) sufficient to assess the forward-looking risk factors affecting the company as of the valuation date?		Identify any analytical gaps you found.	
Are the conclusions presented throughout the appraisal report, including the reconciliation section, relevant and probative of the opined conclusion of value?		Identify any analytical gaps you found.	
Is the appraisal report complete and in accordance with generally accepted appraisal practices in the United States of America?		Does it meet USPAP standards?	
Is the opinion in the appraisal report credible?		Explain the basis for your finding.	

(Continued)

EXHIBIT 5.3   *(Continued)*

Review Criteria	Findings (Pass/Fail)	Comments	Corrective Actions Taken
Would a hypothetical buyer and the hypothetical seller, under the FMV Standard of Value, be willing to purchase and/or sell the appraised interest for the opined amount in the appraisal report?		Explain the basis for your finding.	

As part of your report writing style, use the following powerful phrases and words:

- Ability to replicate information
- Analytical gap
- Appropriateness of the appraisal methods and techniques
- Assess the forward-looking risk factors
- Alternative explanations
- Basis for findings
- Credibility
- General acceptability of chosen methodologies
- Informed judgment
- Lacking in foundation
- Level of care
- Logical connection between the data analyzed and the supporting conclusions
- The opinion of value
- Nonadvocacy
- Probative
- Probative for the purpose of formulating my opinion as expressed in this report
- Proper foundation
- Relevance—relation to the matter at hand
- Reliability—yielding the same results on repeated trials
- Reliably applied
- Supportable opinion
- Should not be construed as an opinion of value
- Transparency
- Reasonable degree of certainty

Also, be sure to avoid weak phrases, such as:

- "It appears"
- "It seems"
- "It could"
- "It looks like"
- "It would seem to me"
- "I don't believe"
- "I believe"
- "Somehow it seems"
- "As if"
- "There appears"
- "It is obvious"
- "It is probable"
- "It is possible"
- "Substantially incorrect"
- "Based on my experience"
- "The appraisal report attempts"
- "Appraisal literature states . . ."
- "That is not the way we do it in our office"
- "The following conclusions can be made"
- "It can be argued"
- ". . . in accordance with authoritative valuation sources"

Avoid references to "in discussion with legal counsel." If you had to seek a legal opinion and you had to incorporate that as part of your review, then clearly say so and state the opinion provided to you as part of your limiting conditions.

 ## STEPPED READING

Read your report the way others might read it, by using stepped reading as a tool for testing your work product for relevancy.

This helps you assess the credibility of your own written opinion. I developed the following technique for reviewing reports. This technique involves reading your own written opinion in nine steps. Each step consists of a "reading" of your work, but with a different objective. As follows:

1. First reading—Concentrate on your table of contents. Does it present a well-defined road map to your reader stakeholders and intended decision makers?

2. Second reading—Concentrate on your conclusions offered in each section of the report, and look for the conclusions in each section that build a nexus to the next logical step in your developmental thought process.

3. Third reading—Did you include appropriate reasonableness tests, and assure yourself that they make sense and are probative of the methodology used?

4. Fourth reading—Did you reconcile the findings presented? Did you include an assessment of each methodology you used, in terms of the quality and the quantity of the data used? Look for a conclusion stating the reasoning for the weights given to each methodology incorporated in the opinion.

5. As you read your report for the third or fourth time, look for gaps among the data, the analysis, and the resulting conclusion(s) at each step of the process presented.

6. By this time, you should be able to assess the sufficiency of the information presented and the general acceptability of the methodology and procedures, given the facts and circumstances of the engagement.

7. Fifth reading—Concentrate on the resources that you provided to allow a reader to replicate the application of your methodology.

8. Look for someone with a similar background as your intended audience, and ask that person to read your report and provide you with objective feedback. Ask that individual to read your report skeptically.

9. Implement changes resulting from these steps, and reread the report following steps 1–8, until you feel comfortable with the results.

Finally, when you read your report, does it depict an independent state of mind, demonstrate acceptance or rejection, and explain your reasoning (i.e., the application of your informed judgment)?

 CONCLUSION

The need to apply informed judgment at the planning phase is put aside many times by the discomfort that an opining individual may experience when making decisions about how to structure a given assignment, given the lack of information at that time. But remember, if you see yourself climbing the Credibility Pyramid, then you should have a basic framework to work with, commencing in the planning phase of an assignment all of the way to the statement and the communication of your opinion to others.

A personal rule that I follow is to allocate 10 to 15 percent of your time on an engagement to planning and related issues. A significant amount of that time should be spent asking questions, researching, and understanding the nature of your client's operations, its history, and its vision. You must apply the same level of intellectual rigor to this phase of an engagement as you do during the application of your methodologies and conclusions.

Chapter 6 discusses reporting and developing your opinion.

NOTES

1. See Rev. Rul. 59–60, 1959-1 CB 237—IRC Sec. 2031. (Also Section 2512.) (Also Part II, Sections 811[k], 1005, Regulations 105, Section 81.10.) Reference(s): Code Sec. 2031 Reg. § 20.2031–2.
2. Jay E. Fishman, Shannon P. Pratt, and William J. Morrison, *Standards of Value: Theory and Applications* (Hoboken, NJ: John Wiley & Sons, 2007), p. 177.

How to Develop and Report Your Opinion

O NE OF THE BEST WAYS to improve your reporting skills is to practice presenting your findings orally by using your written report. You should attempt to do so every time that you write a report. I recommend that when you do so, you use your written report as a script for your oral presentation. You may be surprised at the results.

PRACTICE PRESENTING YOUR WRITTEN FINDINGS ORALLY

Your goal should be to try to use your written report to give an oral presentation, with the challenge before you of explaining your written analytical findings in a relaxed, conversational way.

Once you have managed to orally present all sections of your report, you will need to try to get it down to a 15- to 20-minute speech. One of the benefits of this technique is that you will quickly detect bottlenecks in your analysis, analytical gaps will fly out at you, and you may even decide to change the order of your presentation.

To make this exercise productive, you should attempt it only after you have finished your written report. If you try to do it before you are finished, you may get caught in a loop of paralysis by analysis.

Conversely, every time that you may be tasked to make an oral presentation, you should at least prepare a written summation of your talking points. Then use it to practice from, for your oral presentations. Be mindful of professional standards that address the presentation of oral reports and the required developmental steps that you must follow.

The following oral testimonial summary reflects reporting language used in various sections of a written report that I testified to. I present it here to illustrate the various aspects that a written report should have addressed.

As you can see, this language should naturally flow from the results of your self-assessments presented earlier and be reflective of the contents of the written report:

> My testimony in this case is based on facts and data I found to be sufficient and probative for the purpose of formulating my opinion, as expressed in this report, and is the product of reliable principles and methods, reliably applied to the facts of this case.
>
> The methodologies that I have relied on to form the basis for the expert opinion offered are consistent with similar methodologies and procedures used by valuation analysts performing analyses under similar facts and circumstances and are of a type reasonably relied on by valuation experts in forming opinion or inferences on a subject and have been subjected to peer review and publication.
>
> Furthermore, my testimony concerns matters growing naturally and directly out of the investigations and analyses that I have conducted independent of the litigation.
>
> In formulating a basis for my opinion, I have not extrapolated from an accepted premise to an unfounded conclusion, and I have strived to account for alternative explanations.
>
> I have also established that there is a logical connection between the data I analyzed and the conclusions supporting my opinion of value.
>
> I have applied the same level of care in performing this engagement that I would apply in performing regular professional work outside of litigation consulting.
>
> Business Valuations, as the field of expertise on which I have relied on, is known to reach reliable results for the type of opinion that I am expressing.

In Chapter 5, we discussed the importance of acquired knowledge about your subject, which helps form the basis of your Credibility Pyramid. As we continue with this topic, please refer to the following excerpt from Revenue Ruling 59–60, providing guidance on the minimum elements that should be considered by a valuation analyst:

> The history of a corporate enterprise will show its past stability or instability, its growth or lack of growth, the diversity or lack of diversity of its operations, and other facts needed to form an opinion of the degree of risk involved in the business. For an enterprise, which changed its form of organization but carried on the same or closely similar operations of its predecessor, the history of the former enterprise should be considered. The detail to be considered should increase with approach to the required date of appraisal, since recent events are of greatest help in predicting the future; but a study of gross and net income, and of dividends covering a long prior period, is highly desirable.
>
> The history to be studied should include, but need not be limited to, the nature of the business, its products or services, its operating and investment assets, capital structure, plant facilities, sales records and management, all of which should be considered as of the date of the appraisal, with due regard for recent significant changes. Events of the past that are unlikely to recur in the future should be discounted, since value has a close relation to future expectancy.[1]

No matter the field of endeavor or discipline that you may be opining in, a critical element of your analysis is a thorough knowledge and practical awareness of the nature, history, and outlook of the entity that you are working with. Note that this knowledge and practical awareness encompass not only the enterprise itself, but also the external factors that affect it.

In the following pages, I introduce you to an internal document (as shown in Exhibit 6.1) that I have developed over the years, and that I still use to assist me in acquiring thorough knowledge and practical awareness in any type of engagement. This document is intended to be used as a supplement to any other report-writing checklists, document requests, or any other means that you may already have in place. I have found it to be very useful as an aid in developing the written work product.

EXHIBIT 6.1 Internal Guidance for Establishing an Understanding of the Nature, History, and Outlook of a Subject Company

Item	Element for Inclusion in the Report	Points to Be Discussed in the Written Report	Rev Rule 59–60 Criteria Considered
1	Company Background	The company incorporated on ____ in the state of ____. During the last XXXX years, the company has operated as a XXXXXX. All activity is based in the United States, although a substantial amount of revenues are derived from XXXX sales to international/domestic customers.	History of the company
2	Operations	Describe what the company perceives its main strengths to be:	Understanding the nature of the company
		Well-established, with more than XX years of successful customer-centered operations.	
		Diversified customer-service lines.	
		Excellent track record and relations with customs officials.	
		Logistics support to customers and inventory storage.	
		Describe how the company perceives its main challenge(s) in reacting to changing economic conditions:	
		1.	
		2.	
		3.	
		4.	
		For the year ending December 31, 20XX, the company generated gross sales commissions of approximately $XXX million and employed a workforce of approximately XX individuals, including a sales force of four. Historically, there has been an adequate supply of trained labor.	

	Points to Be Discussed	Rev Rule 59–60 Criteria Considered
3	Management Depth	Assess the level of managerial efficiency below the owner level: Self-sufficient. Highly dependent on the owner. Well trained but not able to execute without the owner. The owners have traditionally worked full time.	Management
4	Capitalization and Stock Ownership	Describe the company's capitalization and stock ownership: The company was a ("C" "S" "partnership" "LLC") from its inception on ____ until XXXX, when it became an "X" corporation. The capitalization consists of XXX class(es) of equity, of XXX five dollar ($X) par value common voting shares of stock authorized, of which XX have been issued and are outstanding as of the valuation date. Since inception ____ shareholders have each owned XX% of the issued and outstanding common stock. As of the valuation date, the common shares issued and outstanding were owned as follows: Individual / Title / Shares owned / As a % of common shares, outstanding	Capital structure
5	Debt to Equity Mix	From a historical perspective, inquire about any plans to change the company's debt/equity ratios. Are there any other plans that may necessitate more borrowing or additional equity capital?	Capital structure

(Continued)

EXHIBIT 6.1 *(Continued)*

		Points to Be Discussed	Rev Rule 59–60 Criteria Considered
6	Products and Services Offered	Describe the nature of the company's products or services, that is, wholesale distribution, retail, industrial equipment, products, logistics and warehousing services, and so on. Summarize, over the last five years, the company's products and services mix along its main natural categories:	Understanding the nature of products and services offered
		Description of product/service line out of 100%:	
		As a percentage of total revenues out of 100%:	
		Does management plan to introduce any new services in the near future?	
		Breakdown of operations:	
		If all domestic, specify geographical areas.	
		If international, specify countries and markets served.	
7	Competition	What is the level of competition at the company's trade level?	Degree of risk involved in the business
		Who are the main competitors?	
		Identify any competitive advantages enjoyed by the company. If there are any, assess them.	
8	Subsidiaries and Affiliates	Identify the affiliated entity or subsidiaries, functions performed.	Nature of the company
		Determine the type and magnitude of activities involved.	
9	Position of the Company Relative to the Industry	How does management assess that the company is positioned within its trade industry sector? Consider the factors affecting the company's ability to provide service to its customers.	Degree of risk involved in the business

10	Regulatory Compliance	Inquire as to the degree that the company's operations are subject to statutory requirements. Were there any known environmental, regulatory, or any other statutory conflicts existing as of the valuation date?	Degree of risk involved in the business
11	Physical Facilities, Capacity, and Business Location	The company occupies a XXXXX-square-foot office warehouse facility, located in XXX, Florida, leased from a related/unrelated entity. Are all of the company's present operations located at this facility? During the site visit, did you inquire whether, as of the valuation date, the present facilities are expected to handle all present and future operational requirements? If not, determine and assess management's plans.	Understanding the nature of the company
12	Sensitivity to Seasonal or Cyclical Factors	Determine whether the company's operations appear to be materially sensitive to seasonal or cyclical factors affecting its industry sectors. Are significant portions of the company's revenues derived from industries whose revenue patterns are tied closely to consumer demand or any other economic factors?	Degree of risk involved in the business
13	Currency and Other Risks	Inquire whether the nature of the company's operations necessitates dealing with currencies other than the U.S. dollar. This could result in the company being exposed to the inherent risks of the international currency markets and foreign governmental regulations. If so, inquire how the company tries to compensate for these exposures. For example, by accelerating any international currency settlements as much as possible and, whenever possible, conducting international transactions in U.S. currency? As of the valuation date, had the company experienced any losses due to its foreign operations?	Degree of risk involved in the business
14	Technology Base	Inquire about management's plans to maintain its information systems, equipment, and technological requirements. Will these efforts result in competitive service advantages in attracting new customers and/or growing any future business opportunities with existing accounts?	Degree of risk involved in the business

(Continued)

EXHIBIT 6.1 (Continued)

		Points to Be Discussed	Rev Rule 59–60 Criteria Considered
15	Dependencies	Is the company dependent on any external factors, such as interest rates, economic factors, and so on, whether local, regional, national, or international in nature and/or scope?	Degree of risk involved in the business
16	Expected Changes in Demand for Products or Services	Inquire whether management is aware of foreseeable or expected changes in the demand for its products or services.	Degree of risk involved in the business
17	External Risks	Is the company exposed to climate risks, due to the geographic characteristics of its operations?	Degree of risk involved in the business
18	Customer Relationships	Describe the company's means of measuring, reporting, and communicating the level of customer satisfaction.	Degree of risk involved in the business
19	Corporate Governance	Has the company publicly communicated its long-term vision statement?	Understanding the nature of the company
20	Corporate Governance	Has the board of directors communicated the strategic objectives that it wants to pursue in the execution of the stated vision?	Understanding the nature of the company
21	Corporate Governance	Has management defined and communicated a methodology for benchmarking the results of its strategic objectives?	Understanding the nature of the company
22	Corporate Governance	Does the company specify strategic goals and objectives and make periodic assessments of any associated risks?	Understanding the nature of the company
23	External Relations	Inquire about relationships affecting operating results and performance, such as alliances, community groups, creditors, gatekeepers, referral sources, vendors, and supply sources.	Understanding the nature of the company

24	Human Capital	Inquire about the skill sets that the company relies on to successfully execute its operations. Does management anticipate any changes in these requirements? Historically, has there been an adequate supply of well-trained personnel to recruit from?	Degree of risk involved in the business
25	Human Capital	Inquire about employee turnover and productivity. Compare company benchmarks for revenue generated by employees with industry benchmarks.	Degree of risk involved in the business
26	Core Competencies	Inquire about management's efforts to define and promote activities critical to the success of the company's operations and profitability. Has management been able to successfully concentrate its efforts on these activities?	Degree of risk involved in the business
27	Corporate Culture	Does management encourage a high level of integrity and ethical behavior? Has an ethics policy been implemented? Does the company have an implemented process to deal with internal conflicts of interest?	Understanding the nature of the company
28	Corporate Culture	Inquire about internal oversight functions monitored by management that are designed to foster accountability and support of the company's operations.	Understanding the nature of the company
29	Laws and Regulations	Inquire about the nature, scope, and impact on the company's operations due to local, state, or national regulations and statutes.	Degree of risk involved in the business
30	Financial Reporting	Inquire about the company's financial reporting system that is in place. Are management reports prepared and distributed on a regular basis?	Degree of risk involved in the business
31	Financial Reporting	Are budgetary reporting systems in place? Are variances from actual operations regularly reviewed and corrective steps implemented?	Degree of risk involved in the business

By now, you have climbed the pyramid and successfully applied your selected methodologies and procedures. As you get ready to formulate your opinion, you need to retrace various aspects of your foundational work. Before you go any further, you need to consider the following eight concepts that can help you build a strong Credibility Pyramid—that is, a strong foundation for your opinion.

1. **Supporting documentation.** Make sure that your work papers and work files clearly point to how your exercise of informed professional judgment was incorporated into your analysis and into your opinion.

2. **Consider your independence during the engagement.** Did any issues arise that impaired your independence? How were those issues resolved? Do you have evidence in your files of the resolution implemented to address any independence issues?

3. **Maintain a high level of professional skepticism as you conduct your engagement.** And just as important, remind your staff to do the same. An easy way to bring to bear the application of professional skepticism within your own firm is to require that your staff support the work undertaken by you. Also, you can implement an internal review process, where individuals in charge of specific portions of an engagement are required to proactively respond to the credibility attributes regarding any conclusions reached prior to the end of the engagement.

4. **Always consider and maintain an awareness of inherent internal inconsistencies in your methodologies and procedures.** Be ready to explain them and demonstrate how the application of your informed professional opinion avoided any analytical gaps or contributed to the reconciliation of these issues. For example, if you calculate a high discount for lack of marketability in the application of an income approach methodology, requiring the calculation of a discount rate, you need to be sure that your risk assessments can be properly reconciled. That is, if, in the same engagement, you derive a low discount rate (implying low risk and resulting in a high valuation), you need to be able to have a connecting nexus to the analysis that is presented to derive a discount for lack of marketability, especially if your discount for lack of marketability implies a high degree of risk inherent in the subject, preventing or hindering its salability. Otherwise, your credibility may be found to be flawed, because your analysis may lack reliability and possibly relevance.

5. **Revisit the stated limiting conditions and assumptions.** Many opining individuals are tempted to use boilerplate language as part of the analysis performed. The author has participated in numerous proceedings where

boilerplate conditions have been at the very core of disputes. Consequently, you should carefully evaluate the appropriateness of your stated limiting conditions and related assumptions as you write the opinion, and you should incorporate a reference to the fact that your opined result is in fact subject to the limiting conditions and assumptions previously presented. A practical tip is to refer to the statement of limiting conditions and assumptions as a "statement of relevant limiting conditions and assumptions," to bring emphasis to the nexus of these limiting conditions to the analysis performed.

You should also read over the various assumptions that are made to make sure that none of them are in contradiction to the analytical process undertaken. For example, if one of your limiting conditions states that the nature of the composition of management will not change as of valuation, but the valuation was prepared for the purpose of liquidating the interest of a partner who will no longer be participating in the management of the enterprise, your assumption will be questioned, and perhaps, rightly so, the credibility of your analysis will be impaired.

6. **Revisit the degree of reliance and relevance of the selected methodologies.** Your opinion is supported by the relevance of the methodologies that you applied to your analytical process. Therefore, you should carefully evaluate the confidence levels that you are willing to attach to your derived results and consider those confidence levels in terms of the quantity and quality of the data that you analyzed.

   Recall that one of the credibility attributes calls for the reliable application of any selected methodologies. Pay particular attention to the various procedural steps performed, as this is where unreliability of results tends to occur, for example, a terminal value calculation that fails to incorporate forecast assumptions.

7. **Consider the impact of others' work on your opined results.** In determination of the value of a business interest, a business valuation analyst may end up relying on the work of other appraisers—for example, real estate appraisers opining on the value of the real estate part of the business interest. In other instances, a valuation may rely on the work of industry specialists or experts to execute some of the procedural appraisal calculations, such as when computing potential inventory obsolescence as a result of changing industry trends.

   When the work of others is part of the foundation supporting your opinion in a material fashion, you should consider the following factors:

   a. **The stated qualifications of the party.** Those qualifications should be analyzed in terms of their probative value for your own foundational work. You should also consider whether that party is independent with respect to the subject matter under consideration.

b. **The magnitude of the opinion you are relying on for the opinion you are proffering.** Back to the example of the business valuation analyst, if the value of the real estate owned by the enterprise being appraised represents most of the value of the business enterprise, perhaps the business valuation analyst should refer the engagement to a real estate appraiser altogether.

c. **The need to disclose the reliance placed on the opinion of others.** Recall that a couple of the operational attributes of credibility that were presented earlier dealt with adequacy of disclosures and transparency. A user of your opined position should be informed of the presence and impact of someone else's work on your foundational work.

8. **Be sure to read and understand the opined work of others that is incorporated into your opinion.** You must understand the scope of the work performed by others, its relevance to your own foundational process, and the completeness of that scope.

   In some instances, you may not be relying on the opinions of others, but you may be relying on published economic and industry research, market data, studies, surveys, and so on. In those instances, at a minimum, you should:

a. Understand the methodology that is used to derive the published results that you have incorporated into your opinion.

b. Consider the general acceptability of those published sources. For example, do other experts in your field also rely on the same sources when performing analytical work under similar facts and circumstances?

 ## VALUATION ADJUSTMENTS

A topical area where many opinions are deficient is in the development of valuation adjustments, such as the discount for lack of marketability and the discount for lack of control. Following is a format that I have used effectively in the past. Note the initial conceptual discussion to acquaint a reader with the concept, followed by a methodology that places the subject company "inside" the studies that were used, as if the company had been a part of the studies.

Also note the discussion of Revenue Ruling 77–287. This should be an essential element in your analysis. The factors enumerated in Revenue Ruling 77–287 are of paramount importance in any derivation of a discount for lack of marketability.

There are many variations of this technique, and, as you can see, the application of your informed judgment will need to be put to good use. The following is presented for illustration purposes only.

Conceptual Framework of Valuation Adjustments

In order to arrive at a supportable opinion of value, a valuation analyst makes reasonable estimates of the nature and magnitude of any valuation adjustments that may be appropriate.

The most common types of valuation adjustments are discounts for lack of control, which address the degree of control, if any, attributable to a particular interest, and discounts for lack of marketability, which address the ability to liquidate an investment in a timely and certain manner. There are no prescribed levels of valuation adjustments; the facts and circumstances of each case should determine the adjustments, if any, to be made on the basis of the level of value obtained from applying the selected valuation methodology.

You should never assume that comments regarding the range or magnitude of any one particular discount or valuation adjustment bear any relevance to your opined conclusion. For example, to say that a certain group of studies or any other form of empirical evidence points to a given range of discounts, in my view, is totally meaningless to your engagement, because you must establish via your analytical process the proper adjustments, if any, to be made in order to derive a credible opinion. While the thought processes and/or conclusions presented in court cases, databases, or empirical studies can be useful tools for your analysis, in and of themselves, they cannot provide you with a credible solution to this dilemma.

As Exhibit 6.2 shows, the primary levels of value—control, marketable minority, and nonmarketable minority—are related to one another by the

EXHIBIT 6.2 Primary Levels of Value

Source: Mercer Capital, www.mercercapital.com

valuation adjustments that are made: control premium, minority interest discount, and marketability discounts.

Premium and discount adjustments derived by a business appraiser are in turn determined by the attributes of the interest to be valued and the resulting financial adjustments made to the economic benefit stream derived by the appraiser. This should only be done after the business appraiser establishes a nexus between the facts and circumstances of the subject and the data or studies used.

One of the methodologies commonly used by valuation analysts to establish a nexus between the facts and circumstances of a subject and the empirical observations found in the professional valuation literature is called *benchmarking*.

Benchmarking methodologies "range from the use of unadjusted averages (not recommended) to qualitative and quantitative adjustments of varying complexity to the averages based on case specific benchmarking with case specific adjustments."[2]

Benchmarking and the empirical data that supports it have been challenged on several grounds. A discussion of some of these criticisms is presented in the following section, as well as an engagement methodology that can be used to overcome these concerns.

Yet before I go any further, let us turn to a conceptual discussion of one of the two main valuation adjustments mentioned: the discount for lack of marketability. Note that the principles discussed equally apply to a derivation of a discount for lack of control.

Discount for Lack of Marketability

I recommend that if you have not read Revenue Ruling 77–287, you do so, and that you readily proceed to incorporate the thought process presented in that revenue ruling into your marketability analysis. In addition, I also recommend that you read the treasury publication *Discount for Lack of Marketability Job Aid for IRS Valuation Professionals*. The publication can be found at www.valfor.net/downloads.php.

The discount for lack of marketability encompasses two interrelated impairments to value:

1. Lack of prompt salability, and
2. The lack of liquidity resulting from the inability to achieve a prompt sale. Revenue Ruling 77–287 deals with the valuation of securities restricted from immediate resale and amplifies Revenue Ruling 59–60 by providing further guidelines for the valuation, for federal tax purposes, of securities that cannot be immediately resold because they are restricted from resale pursuant to federal securities laws.

Revenue Ruling 77–287 proposed several factors as indicative of the magnitude of valuation adjustments that may be required on a case-specific basis:

a. **Earnings.** Earnings and sales consistently have a significant influence on the size of restricted securities discounts, according to the study. Earnings played a major part in establishing the ultimate discounts at which these stocks were sold from the current market price. Apparently, earnings patterns, rather than sales patterns, determine the degree of risk of an investment.

b. **Sales.** The dollar amount of sales of issuers' securities also has a major influence on the amount of discount at which restricted securities sell from the current market price. The results of the study generally indicate that the companies with the lowest dollar amount of sales during the test period accounted for most of the transactions involving the highest discount rates, while they accounted for only a small portion of all transactions involving the lowest discount rates.

c. **Trading market.** The market in which publicly held securities are traded also reflects variances in the amount of discount that is applied to restricted securities purchases. According to the study, discount rates were greatest on restricted stocks with unrestricted counterparts traded over the counter, followed by those with unrestricted counterparts listed on the American Stock Exchange, while the discount rates for stocks with unrestricted counterparts listed on the New York Stock Exchange were the smallest.

d. **Resale agreement provisions**. Resale agreement provisions often affect the size of the discount. The discount from the market price provides the main incentive for a potential buyer to acquire restricted securities. In judging the opportunity cost of freezing funds, the purchaser is analyzing two separate factors. The first factor is the risk that the underlying value of the stock will change in a way that, absent the restrictive provisions, would prompt a decision to sell.

Public shares, actively and freely traded on an exchange or over the counter, provide both immediate salability and liquidity; however, most closely held interests do not enjoy such a degree of liquidity. It is generally accepted among valuation analysts that Revenue Ruling 77–287 acknowledges the need for consideration of a lack of marketability in the valuation of a not freely marketable, closely held business interest.[3]

Therefore, a valuation analyst looks for appropriate methodologies in an attempt to quantify these differences in liquidity. A discount for lack of marketability is used by valuation analysts in an attempt to estimate the effect on value caused by the inability to liquidate a closely held interest as quickly as a publicly traded security.[4]

Whether an interest is privately held or publicly traded affects the value of the interest to both a hypothetical buyer and hypothetical seller under the fair market value standard.

All other factors being equal, an interest traded in a public market, generally, is worth more than one not traded in a public market. An ownership interest in a closely held entity cannot be liquidated as readily as a similar interest in a publicly traded company.

This difference in liquidity is regarded by investors as an added risk factor inherent in closely held interests, which translates to a decrease in value of an otherwise equal but not publicly traded interest. The subject is not publicly registered, and neither a public nor a secondary trading market exists for the timely execution of a sale or a trade of an interest in the subject.

This inability to readily sell an interest in the subject increases a hypothetical buyer's exposure to changing market conditions and increases the ownership risk of the hypothetical seller. Because of the lack of marketability and the resulting increased risk associated with ownership of a closely held interest, a hypothetical buyer would demand a higher return or yield in comparison to a similar but publicly traded interest, and a hypothetical seller would be willing to accept the resulting lower return.

The quantification of this decrease in value, which may be attributable to the lack of liquidity inherent in ownership of a closely held interest, is the process valuation that analysts use in order to assess the impact on value. Certain factors are generally accepted by valuation analysts as determinants of the magnitude of a discount for lack of marketability.[5]

You should also keep in mind that your analysis needs to consider the characteristics of the marketplace where the subject interest valued is considered to be sold on the basis of the engagement's applicable standard of value.

 ## DESCRIPTION OF A BENCHMARKING METHODOLOGY USED BY VALUATION ANALYSTS

There are four major problems associated with the restricted stock studies. First, shares analyzed in the restricted stock studies differ from shares in closely held companies in a number of important ways, including: a known limited holding period, financial reporting transparency, and the liquidity of the public market. Second, the discounts identified in the studies fell in a very wide range (for example, the Management Planning study discounts ranged from zero to 57.6 percent). Third, many of these studies do not provide detailed information on each of the transactions included in the study. Lastly, a number of these studies are more than thirty years old.[6]

In addressing the comparability and relevance concerns previously mentioned, analysts select empirical studies that are considered relevant and comparable to the subject under consideration. Keep in mind that there are many methodologies used by valuation analysts to derive a discount for lack of marketability. They range from various quantitative models to benchmarking. In my view, they all share some degree of lack of relevancy issues to a not freely marketable subject interest; which means that no matter how you select to do it, this is a part of the valuation process that will require an analyst to bring to the table a great deal of informed judgment in reaching a conclusion on the degree of marketability affecting the valuation conclusion. As an independent analyst, you will have to determine which techniques are most appropriate when climbing the Credibility Pyramid. Personally, I prefer a benchmarking technique combined with an intensive analysis of the facts and circumstances affecting the subject interest under consideration. Note that in my view, benchmarking must be supported by a concurrent intensive relevant qualitative analysis, otherwise the result will not be credible. For this discussion and an illustration of a benchmarking methodology, I am going to select two restricted stock studies: the Management Planning, Inc., study and the Johnson/Park study.

The methodology that was used consisted of determining the factors in each study that had the greatest potential for identifying variables with a clear tendency to confirm expectations regarding a discount for lack of marketability and that seemed to be the most predictive of their magnitude.

The variables affecting the degree of marketability indicated by the two selected published restricted stock studies were then applied to the subject, in order to provide benchmarks for a range of probable discounts for lack of marketability. Consequently, the derived averaged benchmark, based on the application of the case-specific facts and circumstances of the engagement, established a nexus between the subject and the empirical observations concluded in the selected studies.

In addition, I also considered several qualitative factors, established by generally accepted business valuation practices and by Revenue Rulings 59–60 and 77–287, as relevant qualitative factors in determining a discount for lack of marketability, because additional benchmarks were indicative of a probable

EXHIBIT 6.3 Summary Statistics

Statistic	Restricted Stock Discount	Revenues (mils)	Recent Earnings (mils)	Market Capitalization (mils)	Value of Shares Sold (mils)
Mean	27.7%	$ 47.5	$ 2.1	$ 80.4	$ 9.5
Median	28.1%	$ 29.8	$ 0.7	$ 43.5	$ 4.9
Minimum	0.0%	$ 3.2	$ 0.1	$ 3.4	$ 0.4
Maximum	57.6%	$ 293.0	$ 24.0	$ 686.5	$ 100.0

discount for lack of marketability relevant to the subject to the extent that their possible impact on the subject had not been incorporated into the derivation of the discount rate or the benefit stream or otherwise made part of the methodologies previously employed.[7]

Management Planning, Inc., Study

Management Planning, Inc. (MPI) studied private placements for the period between 1980 and 1996. The mean and median discounts were 27.7 percent and 28.8 percent, respectively. Exhibit 6.3 provides summary statistics.

MPI found five variables that had a clear tendency to confirm expectations regarding discounts for lack of marketability and that seemed to be the most predictive of their magnitude:

1. **Revenues.** Higher revenues, lower discounts
2. **Recent earnings.** Higher earnings, lower discounts
3. **Market price/share.** Higher prices, lower discounts
4. **Price stability.** Higher stability, lower discounts
5. **Earnings stability.** Higher stability, lower discounts

MPI broke down the observed discount for each of these five factors as follows in Exhibit 6.4. Note that the applicable metrics for the subject are reported in the last column, as if the subject company was a part of the study.

As to revenues, the subject's most recent revenue level placed it in the third quartile; on this basis, the median 3rd quartile finding of 31.5 percent was selected. A second variable in the study, earnings, was found to be relevant to the subject. Our analysis of the subject's dividend-paying capacity indicates an average dividend payout ratio of approximately 90 percent. Under these conditions, a hypothetical buyer of a minority interest in the

EXHIBIT 6.4 MPI Observed Discounts for the Five Factors

| Variable/Ranking | Statistic | Restricted Stock Discount | | | | Subject |
		1st Quartile	2nd Quartile	3rd Quartile	4th Quartile	
Revenues	Median	18.7%	22.2%	31.5%	36.6%	**31.5%**
(highest to lowest)	Mean	21.8%	23.9%	31.9%	34.7%	
Earnings	Median	16.1%	30.5%	32.7%	39.4%	**16.1%**
(highest to lowest)	Mean	18.0%	30.0%	30.1%	34.1%	
Market Price/Share	Median	23.3%	22.2%	29.5%	41.0%	**N/A**
(highest to lowest)	Mean	23.3%	24.5%	27.3%	37.3%	
Price Stability	Median	34.6%	31.6%	19.2%	19.4%	**N/A**
(lowest to highest)	Mean	34.8%	33.3%	21.0%	22.0%	
Earnings Stability	Median	14.1%	26.2%	30.8%	44.8%	**14.1**
(highest to lowest)	Mean	16.4%	28.8%	27.8%	39.7%	
Management Planning Inc. (MPI) study—calculated average for subject						**20.6%**

subject would enjoy a high degree of liquidity in the form of "S" dividend distributions. On this basis, we selected the 1st quartile categories of the MPI study for an indication of the discount for lack of marketability. Finally, a third variable in the study, earnings stability, was determined to be relevant to the subject. As indicated in Section 4.3, Analysis of Operations, the company's profitability consistently exceeded the industry's for every one of the years reviewed. Therefore, on this basis, the subject was ranked in the 1st quartile category of the MPI study for an indication of the discount for lack of marketability. Therefore, the MPI study findings, when applied to the subject company, would indicate an average discount for lack of marketability of 20.6 percent for the subject.

Johnson/Park Study

Johnson and Park examined three factors that affected the magnitude of the discount: sales (higher sales, lower discounts); net income (higher earnings, lower discounts); and transaction size (larger transactions, lower discounts). Their findings are shown in Exhibit 6.5.

EXHIBIT 6.5 Study Findings

Average Discount	Sales (mils)	Average Discount	Transaction Size (mils)
23.5%	$0 to $10	**26.7%**	$0 to $5
19.4%	$10 to $50	20.9%	$5 to $10
17.7%	$50 to $200	17.0%	$10 to $25
13.0%	Over $200	10.8%	Over $25
Average Discount	Net Income (mils)	Average Discount	Net Income Margin
22.5%	Negative	22.5%	Negative
26.0%	$0 to $1	23.7%	0% to 5%
18.1%	$1 to $10	**15.2%**	5% to 10%
6.3%	Over $10	11.6%	Over 10%

The bold numbers are the values of the subject company.

These factors were found to be relevant to the subject; thus, the application of these factors to the subject, i.e., as if the Subject had been a part of the original study, is shown in Exhibit 6.6.

Therefore, the Johnson/Park study findings, when applied to the subject company, would indicate an average discount for lack of marketability of 19.90 percent for the subject.

Note that at this point in our analysis of the marketability attributes of this subject interest, I have basically placed the subject company in the selected empirical studies. One caveat to remember is that you will need to establish that the selected empirical studies are similar enough to your subject company in order to derive a meaningful conclusion. Your analysis will need to identify

EXHIBIT 6.6 Application of Johnson Park Study Findings to the Subject

Relevant Factor Reported by the Johnson Park/Study	Financial Metric Relevant to the Subject	Average Discount for Lack of Marketability Reported by the Johnson/Park Study
Sales	$10 to $50 million	19.40%
Net income	Zero to $1 million	26.00%
Net income margin	5% to 10%	15.20%
	Average discount—all factors selected when applied to the subject	19.90%

those factors that you considered to have established that level of similarity between your subject company and those in the empirical study.

 ## BENCHMARKING: RELATIVE WEIGHTS AND QUALITATIVE ANALYSIS

The following information is sourced from a presentation at the 2002 National Conference of the Institute of Business Appraisers by Richard L. Schwartz, CBA, ASA, CPA/ABV, CFE:

> In the calculation of an applicable discount for lack of marketability, we also considered the following qualitative nine factors, generally accepted by valuation analysts as having the greatest potential for identifying those variables with a clear tendency to confirm expectations regarding a discount for lack of marketability, and which seemed to be the most predictive of their magnitude when deriving a discount for lack of marketability for the Subject.
>
> The range of numerical values assigned to each qualitative factor serves to indicate a possible range of discounts for lack of marketability that could be applied to a subject based on indications from empirical studies and current trends in business valuation practices.
>
> The specific numerical values assigned below represent the appraiser's informed judgment of each factor in comparison to the two restricted stock studies determined to be relevant to the Subject:
>
> - **Dividend policy.** A higher rate of return earned by a hypothetical investor over a given holding period would call for a lower discount for lack of marketability. Such an investor would enjoy significant liquidity over the period of ownership in addition to any possible long term gains realized upon a future sale of the stock. These circumstances point to a lower marketability discount than the study findings. An analysis of the Subject's dividend capacity can be found in Section 4.6, which indicates an average payout ratio of 90% over the past four years. On this basis, we assigned a lower rating from the combined study findings of –3.
> - **Size of the interest.** Since the interest being valued is less than necessary to establish operational control, the interest may not be as liquid, indicating an equal or greater marketability discount

than the combined study findings. On this basis, we assigned a rating from the combined study findings of +2.

■ **Restriction on transfer.** If restrictions on transfers limit the price and term of payment to be received, then a potential hypothetical investor would consider these restrictions as increasing the lack of marketability. As of the Valuation date, the controlling shareholder was executing plans to severely restrict a future transfer of the interest being valued. Therefore, a higher marketability discount than the study findings would be indicated. On this basis, we assigned a higher rating from the combined study findings of +2.

■ **Access to reliable information and quality of management.** Management shares financial information with its shareholders on a timely basis. Therefore, a hypothetical buyer would consider an interest in the Subject at least equally marketable with those in the two studies, indicating a discount for lack of marketability equal to or less than the study findings. On this basis, we assigned a rating equal to the combined study findings.

■ **Financial statement analysis.** An independent CPA audits the Subject's financial statements annually, and also, monthly interim financial statements are compiled. The Company has an excellent reputation in the industry and its financial ratios compare favorably with those of the industry. *Inasmuch as these factors were already considered in the derivation of the discount rate and in the financial assessment of the subject, we assigned a rating equal to the combined study findings.*

■ **"Put" rights/redemption policy.** A put right can guarantee a market under certain conditions and is considered one of the most important factors that could reduce a discount for lack of marketability. However, the Company has no history of buying back any of its shares and as of the valuation date, there were no plans to redeem any shares and no plans existed for a redemption or put policy. Therefore, a hypothetical buyer would consider an interest in the Subject significantly less marketable, indicating a discount for lack of marketability greater than the study findings. On this basis, we assigned a higher rating from the combined study findings of +3.

■ **Potential buyers.** There are no potential buyers and no transactions have occurred in the past, therefore, marketability would be limited, and a marketability discount equal to or greater than the study findings would be indicated since the shares of the companies in the restricted stock studies are publicly traded. On this basis, we assigned a rating greater than the combined study findings of +3.

▪ **Entity size relative to the industry.** Since the Company's competitors tend to be larger in size, the Company's visibility in the industry may be limited and therefore considered less marketable. However, despite its size, the Subject's client list includes a significant number of major airlines and public companies. Therefore, on this basis, we assigned a rating greater than the combined study findings of +2.

▪ **Revenue Ruling 59–60.** A hypothetical buyer would consider the nature of the Company's business, its history, position relative to industry peers, and the impact of the economy on the Subject as determinants of value. Our evaluation of the Subject concluded that the Company is stable and fairly diverse; however, the Company is also subject to fluctuations in the economy and aircraft industry trends. *Inasmuch as these factors were already considered in the derivation of the discount rate and in the financial assessment of the subject, we assigned a rating equal to the combined study findings.*

▪ **Prospect of a public offering and costs or sale of the business (holding period)**. The longer the perceived holding period to which an investment is subject, the greater probability that market risk is likely to impact the value of the Subject. Therefore, since the Subject has no plans to offer an initial public offering and the Company is not being considered for sale, a hypothetical buyer considering the potential for an extended holding period would require an equal or greater discount than the study findings since liquidity would not be imminent. However, since the Subject's dividend payment history indicates an average payout ratio of 90%, a hypothetical buyer could expect to receive a significant amount of liquidity during the extended holding period. On this basis, we assigned a higher rating from the combined study findings of +3.

These findings are summarized in Exhibit 6.7.

The net result from the "Relative Weights and Qualitative Analysis" indicates a factor of +12 to be added to the study findings.

Conclusion and Summation of Factors

Applying the relevant factors to the subject from the selected studies, while considering the qualitative factors that could be expected to increase or decrease the amount of the discount for lack of marketability to the subject interest,

EXHIBIT 6.7 Applicable Discount for Lack of Marketability

	Subtract from Study Findings				Study Findings	Add to Study Findings			
Factors	−4	−3	−2	−1		+1	+2	+3	+4
1. Dividend Policy, Payments, and Yield	x								
2. Size of Interest						x			
3. Restriction on Transfer						x			
4. Access to Reliable Information and Quality of Company Management					x				
5. Financial Statement Analysis					x				
6. "Put" Rights/Redemption Policy								x	
7. Potential Buyers								x	
8. Entity Size Relative to Industry						x			
9. Revenue Ruling 59–60, Economic Outlook, Nature of Business					x				
10. Prospect of Public Offering and Costs or Sale of Business (Holding Period)								x	
Totals		−3			N/A			+6	+9

we were able to reasonably estimate a discount for lack of marketability of 32 percent. These findings were consistent with those of the selected studies, namely:

> smaller companies generally have larger discounts for lack of marketability. Since historical returns indicate that smaller companies are riskier than larger companies, an implication can be made that the discount for lack of marketability increases as the risk of the subject company increases. A similar conclusion resulted when the companies were examined based on the level of net income. A higher discount for lack of marketability was observed for companies with lower levels of positive net income.[8]

Finally, the effect of the discount for lack of marketability was tested in the sanity check performed later in Section 11.2, where an internal rate of return was computed after deriving an indication of value resulting from the application of a discount for lack of marketability, as indicated below.

A summary of the overall findings is presented here:

Economic analysis based on comparison of subject to MPI study	20.6%
Economic analysis based on comparison of subject to Johnson/Park study	19.9%
Average of MPI and Johnson/Park study findings applied to subject	20.0% (average)
Net result from relative weights and qualitative analysis	+12.0%
Discount for lack of marketability (rounded)	32% (rounded)

Making Sure Your Opinion Is Assessed as Credible

The important elements of the previously referenced benchmarking technique are

1. The results can be duplicated.
2. There is transparency of the information presented.
3. Informative disclosures are provided.
4. The application of the valuation analyst's informed judgment is clearly and concisely presented. No black boxes.

Now let us return to a couple more factors that you should consider to make sure that your opinion will be assessed as credible.

MAKE SURE THERE ARE NO ANALYTICAL GAPS IN THE DEVELOPMENT AND DERIVATION OF GROWTH RATES

The derivation of a growth rate is another area where the application of informed judgment will be required and expected by the stakeholders and one where valuation analysts seem to struggle and have difficulties.

The easiest approach to the derivation of a growth rate is to start out with the macro economic factors and industry considerations and finish with an assessment of your subject's resources, capacities, and capabilities as of the valuation date. When deriving a growth rate, your financial analysis needs to be detailed enough to make a case for the proffered growth rate. Be very mindful of analytical gaps. It is common for growth rates to be unsupported by the

EXHIBIT 6.8a Integra Information—Gross Domestic Product and Inflation Growth Indicators

Gross Domestic Product (GDP) & Inflation Growth Indicators					
Historical	GDP	Inflation	Forecasted	GDP	Inflation
2005	6.5%	3.0%	2010	3.9%	1.5%
2006	6.0%	2.7%	2011	3.5%	2.4%
2007	5.1%	2.7%	2012	5.6%	2.7%
2008	2.6%	3.3%	2013	5.9%	2.9%
2009	−1.5%	−0.4%	2014	5.2%	3.0%

EXHIBIT 6.8b Integra Information— Historical Industry versus Forecasted Industry Revenue Growth

	Revenue Growth				
	Historical	Industry	Subject	Forecasted	Industry
	2005	10.3%	37.5%	2010	1.2%
	2006	8.2%	8.1%	2011	2.2%
	2007	10.4%	−2.7%	2012	4.6%
	2008	4.3%	28.1%	2013	4.1%
	2009	5.5%	−21.7%	2014	3.9%
Averages		7.7%	9.9%		3.2%

Source: "Industry Growth Outlook Report" for Computer Systems Design Services, published by Microbilt Corporation's Integra Financial Benchmarking Data ("Integra"), 2009.

results and conclusions drawn from the financial analysis that is presented and other sections of the analysis that are undertaken. Also, it is very helpful to present the company's actual historical growth record, next to the industry's historical growth record, together with the prospective outlooks for both the industry and the subject.

As depicted in Exhibits 6.8a, 6.8b, and 6.9, industry revenue growth is forecasted to average approximately 3.2 percent for the period 2010–2014. This forecasted industry revenue growth is predicated on the economy achieving a forecasted 3.9 percent growth in 2010 GDP and averaging 5.05 percent thereafter for the following four years, economic levels that may be difficult to achieve, assuming the economic outlook.

Be careful not to confuse an industry's growth, which is typically stated in terms of sales or revenue growth, with a growth rate for a different benefit

EXHIBIT 6.9 Apply the Growth Rate Assumptions

Fiscal Year Ending	Most Recent Year's Gross Revenues	Forecasted Integra Industry Annual Growth Rate	Resulting Subject's Forecasted (Based on Integra Growth Rates) Revenues	Independent Management's Sales Forecast	Management's versus Integra's Forecast: Resulting Variances	Management's Forecast Trend	Forecasted Discretionary Earnings Based on Management's Forecasts
12/31/2009	$2,287,028						
12/31/2010		1.20%	2,314,472	2,491,811	177,339	Positive	299,017
12/31/2011		2.20%	2,365,391	2,395,000	29,609	Neutral	287,400
12/31/2012		4.60%	2,474,199	2,417,000	−57,199	Negative	290,040
12/31/2013		4.10%	2,575,641	2,434,000	−141,641	Negative	292,080
12/31/2014		3.90%	2,676,091	2,455,000	−221,091	Negative	294,600
Forward Looking Averages		3.20%	2,481,159	2,438,562	−42,596		292,627

stream, other than sales or revenues. You need to calculate the effect that a forecasted growth rate in revenues will have on the benefit stream that you are going to use as part of the indication of value. Many valuation reports make the egregious mistake of interchanging growth rates without considering the level of the stated benefit stream.

And then, from this information, proceed to apply the growth rate assumptions to the subject company, as follows in Exhibit 6.9. In addition, the valuation analyst also analyzed the company in comparison to its industry peers, in terms of the forecasted annual sustainable growth rate of the subject versus its industry peers.

In conclusion, the immediate future for the Computer Systems Design & Integration Services industry sector looks like a period of tough belt tightening and low single-digit growth, averaging approximately 3.2%, provided that the forecasted economic levels previously mentioned can be attained.

As can be seen previously, during the five-year forward future term, the resulting differences are not significant and point to the subject's expected level of operating performance being at or near those of its industry peers.

Growth forecasts should be reviewed in conjunction with the related inherent industry risk/volatility so that an assessment of the likely attainment of forecasted growth levels can be made in light of the attending risk levels attributed to a particular industry. You can test the inherent industry risk by plotting the Ibbotson industry premia, as in the following example.[9]

	Published Industry Premia	No. of Companies Surveyed	Ibbotson Page No.	SIC
Year 2001	5.6	672	48	737
Year 2004	6.9	141	52	7373
Year 2007	2.7	111	53	7373
Year 2009	−.80	91	40	7373

The appraiser then proceeded to graph the above data, including a related linear trend line. Exhibit 6.10 depicts the relationship of industry risk premia, as published by Ibbotson and Associates, over time. This data points to a material decrease in industry risk, which implies a positive likelihood of the company's expected performance being at or near industry levels.

Finally, you could summarize your thought process in reaching the aforementioned long-term sustainable growth rate conclusion, as shown in Exhibit 6.11.

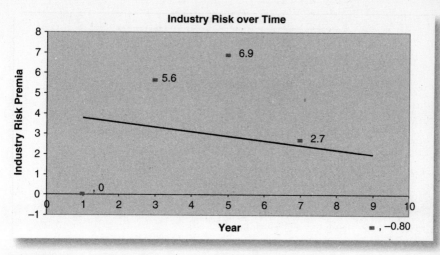

EXHIBIT 6.10 Relationship of Industry Risk Premia Over Time

Source: Industry risk premia obtained from Ibbotson *SBBI 2010 Valuation Yearbook*. Copyright © 2010, 2008, 2005, 2002.

EXHIBIT 6.11 Appraiser's Thought Process in Determining Applicable Growth Rate

Factors Considered	Discussed in	Impact on Growth Rate
Subject's historical growth trends	Sections 3.3.2 and 3.4.1	Upward
Management's current expectations as to future growth	Section 3.9	Improving
Economic factors affecting the Subject's operations	Sections 2.2 and 3.4	Improving

Whenever you are attempting to derive a growth rate, you might find it useful to think of the process as an inverted pyramid. See Exhibit 6.12.

INCORPORATING PROSPECTIVE INFORMATION THAT IS PRESENTED INTO YOUR OPINED RESULTS

Many practitioners take the view that as long as management prepares any type of prospective information, their responsibility over such matters is then limited. However, I do not agree with that view.

I would suggest to you that at the time that you incorporate into your analytical process any information provided to you, regardless of the type,

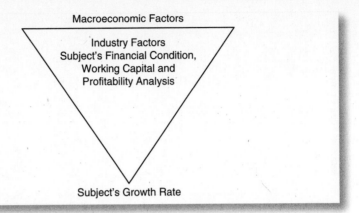

EXHIBIT 6.12 Deriving a Growth Rate

historical or prospective, or where it came from, from that moment on, you own it! Think of it this way: such information now becomes part of the foundational aspects of your opinion. Therefore, act accordingly, affording it the due professional care required, because you will need to develop precise and concise forecasting assumptions.

In the following pages is a sample set of forecast assumptions for a discounted cash flow methodology. Note the references to the economic and industry and financial analysis as incorporated into the forecasted presentation.

Forecasted Financial Operations and Assumptions: Multiple Period Discounting Method

A subject's forecasted financial performance is typically assessed in terms of the effects of inflation, economic and industry outlooks, potential growth of product sales levels, and the resulting effects on the firm's net cash flows.

It is a generally accepted view among valuation analysts that products normally go through a life cycle encompassing four distinct phases: introduction, growth, maturity, and decline. Therefore, it is important to understand which life cycle best represents a subject's products as of the valuation date, and, based on that observation, an appropriate assumption can be made regarding the expected growth of product sales levels. On that basis, a forecast of future sales levels can be built on the observation that the subject's product cycle, as defined by the industry data, as of the valuation date, is best described as matured, growing, declining, or at an introductory phase.

Furthermore, the industry outlook also needs to be considered to determine whether it points to falling product prices, perhaps because of new competitors entering that industry sector. During the maturity stage, competition is based primarily on price and perceived differences in product quality and service. Prices are generally stable throughout this phase and usually go up only at an inflationary rate, all factors indicative of a moderate single-digit sustainable growth rate.

A forecast period typically extends through the terminal year after a stabilized level of operations is estimated to be attained. As a basis for forecasting, a valuation analyst interprets the effect of key economic and industry factors and management's future expectations on the subject. For example, see the following forecast narrative:

- A material decline in the forecasted 2013 sales revenues and net cash flow levels, as compared to the levels attained during 2012.
- Forecasted 2013 operations and net cash flow levels can be expected to be similar to the levels attained during 2012.
- Forecasted 2014 operations and net cash flow levels can be expected to be similar to levels attained during 2011, rather than the predicted industry levels. We based this assumption on the fact that management's sales forecast for 2013 indicates a decrease of 30.33 percent from the sales level attained in 2011 and a 40.94 percent decrease from the sales level attained in 2010. Therefore, we find it doubtful that the subject would be able to experience a 20 percent increase in sales during a two-year period.
- Forecasted 2015 sales revenues, and thereafter, are expected to increase at a 5 percent growth rate, supported by a 3 percent annual growth in the gross domestic product and 2 percent inflation. (See Section X.X.)

Due to the increasing need to keep up with the latest technological trends, a company may need to plan for continuing capital expenditures. Unless otherwise indicated, the forecasts should be based on assumptions of normalized future operations and should be presented on the same accounting basis used by the subject company.

Forecasted future net cash flow, derived in the development of the present values of future operations and of the terminal value, can then be computed. These values should be the result of data provided by the company and its management and should be based on assumptions and estimates assessed by the valuation analyst. Management needs to agree to the reasonableness of any assumptions used. In addition, remember that any forecast is also based on the analyst's knowledge and beliefs as of the valuation date about the company's future operations, in addition to any estimates made by management.

In the final analysis, the forecast should represent the future expected results of operations, the resulting financial condition, cash flow based on the company's existing business plans as of the valuation date; however, the ultimate outcome of any of the assumptions used may differ materially from the results forecasted. Consequently, you must apply your informed judgment together with a healthy dose of professional skepticism when considering the risks associated with any forecast presented.

All forecasts that are presented should be included solely to assist in the development of the value conclusion presented in the valuation report, and they should not be used for any other purpose. If appropriate, you may wish to indicate that these presentations necessarily are not intended to include all of the disclosures required by the guidelines established by the American Institute of Certified Public Accountants for the presentation of a financial forecast and that the actual results may vary from the forecasts presented, and the variations may be material.

At a minimum, the following foundational factors or assumptions for a typical forecast are as follows:

- **Forecasted sales and cost of goods sold.** Forecasted first year's gross sales in the amount of $7,600,000 were used on the basis of information provided by management and supported by the economic and industry outlooks. The first year's forecasted sales represent a XX.XX percent decline in gross sales, when compared to the sales reported by the subject for the year 2001. In addition, sales for the subsequent years were also determined on the application of the industry and economic outlook to the operations of the subject, which indicates a forecasted return to the 2001 levels achieved by the year 2004, and thereafter a 5 percent sustainable growth rate in gross sales was forecasted, resulting in the following levels of forecasted sales:

  Year 2003: $7,600,000
  Year 2004: $10,080,000
  Year 2005: $15,100,000
  Year 2006: $15,855,000
  Year 2007: $16,648,000
  Year 2008: $17,480,000

Year 2009: $18,354,000
Year 2010: $19,272,000
Year 2011: $20,235,000
Year 2012: $21,247,000

Cost of goods sold is expected to remain stable as a result of management's continuing efforts to offset declining industry gross margins. The forecast assumes that the subject would pass on any upward pressure on costs to its customers. A forecasted cost of goods sold of 74.5 percent was used, which is in line with the company's operations as of the valuation date, as well as the industry outlook and future management's expectations.

▪ **Capital expenditures versus depreciation.** The forecast assumes that 2003 capital expenditures will be a sum of $261,655 and thereafter will continue to grow at an annual rate of 2 percent over the previous year. On this basis, capital expenditures are estimated to exceed depreciation charges by a factor of approximately 21 percent. The published work of Gilbert E. Mathews indicates that on average, a growing company experiencing a 5 percent real growth rate, would be expected to experience a 19.4 percent excess of capital expenditures over depreciation, assuming straight line depreciation methods.[10] The subject's forecasted 21 percent excess of capital expenditures over depreciation charges is consistent with the industry outlook, which indicates that above-average levels of capital resources will need to be committed by industry participants in order to remain technologically competitive. During our tour of the company's premises, management indicated that present plant capacity was adequate to sustain long-term growth prospects without the need to replace or procure any additional major capital assets, and no impaired or idled assets were observed. Management was in agreement with the level of forecasted capital expenditures.

▪ **General and administrative expenses.** General and administrative expenses were projected at 19.2 percent of forecasted sales. This level of expenditures is in line with historical operating expense levels and compares favorably with industry data. As of the valuation date, no changes in this relationship were expected; therefore, general and administrative expenses were assumed to grow at the indicated rate of 19.2 percent of forecasted sales.

▪ **Forecasted cash used to decrease debt balances.** Although a certain level of debt is common to the industry, the forecast assumes that capital expenditures and future working capital requirements are to be funded from operations; therefore, the only change in debt would be a normal reduction of principal and interest payments. On this basis, annual principal reductions of $60,000 per year were calculated based on the company's outstanding debt balances and borrowing practices as of the valuation date.

■ **Forecasted cash needed to support working capital.** The forecasted cash levels needed to support working capital levels were based on an analysis of management's future requirements to maintain an adequate level of liquidity to operate the company and are consistent with the conclusions reached in the financial analysis of the subject. On this basis, normalized working capital, as of the valuation date, was then affected by the projected changes in cash estimated to be needed to support future operations during the forecast periods. See Exhibit 6.13.

■ **Net cash flow to equity holders.** The resulting 6 percent forecasted growth in net cash flow that was projected to be available to the equity holders was calculated after considering the operating characteristics and the forecasted capital expenditures of the subject, as follows in Exhibit 6.14.

EXHIBIT 6.13   Projected Changes in Cash Needed

Forecast Period	Forecasted Additional Cash Needed to Support Working Capital ($)	Forecasted Working Capital as a Percentage of Forecasted Sales (%)
Year 2003	7,600	23.31
Year 2004	6,144	22.86
Year 2005	45,300	15.96
Year 2006	3,171	15.60
Year 2007	124,858	15.60
Year 2008	61,180	15.62
Year 2009	27,531	15.62
Year 2010	84,796	15.62
Year 2011	40,471	15.60
Year 2012	131,733	15.60

EXHIBIT 6.14 Cash Flow Projected Available

Projected as a Percentage of Net Cash Forecasted					
Flow in Sales					
Year 2003	$419,000	4.36%	Year 2008	$851,000	4.87%
Year 2004	$450,000	4.46%	Year 2009	$937,000	5.11%
Year 2005	$725,000	4.80%	Year 2010	$935,000	4.85%
Year 2006	$812,000	5.12%	Year 2011	$1,038,000	5.13%
Year 2007	$738,000	4.43%	Year 2012	$1,007,000	4.74%

- **Term of the forecast.** The forecast of net cash flow covers the future years, which, in the opinion of the appraiser, will be necessary to achieve a stabilized level of operations based on the conclusions and the analysis of the economic and industry outlook and management's expectations as of the valuation date. On this basis, it was projected that a stabilized level of operations would be reached in the year 2010, and the terminal year is therefore 2011, which represents the first full year of stabilized operations.
- **Terminal value.** In order to calculate the total value of the interest, an assumption is made as if a hypothetical sale of the business interest occurs after achieving a sustainable and constant level of benefits. The present value of the future hypothetical amount realized from the hypothetical sale is called *terminal value*. In order to estimate the value at the time of the hypothetical future sale, the forecasted benefit stream—in this case, net cash flow to equity holders—is converted into an estimate of value by applying a capitalization rate of 17 percent, as determined in Section 9.2.6.
- **Mid-year convention.** An analysis of the subject's cash flow and cash dividend distribution practices indicated that these returns to equity holders, historically, have been distributed over the fiscal periods more so on a proportional basis than at the end of each period. Therefore, a mid-year convention was used in the discounting of these types of cash flow.
- **Keep in mind the difference between a "forecast" and a "projection."** A *forecast* is defined as the most likely or expected outcome. Therefore, in a business valuation engagement, the conditions existing as of the valuation

date are forecasted on the basis of a *most likely or expected outcome* for valuation purposes and not on a "what-if" basis, unless the premise of the valuation is to establish the value of a company under those what-if conditions, which makes a hypothetical valuation.

A *projection*, conversely, involves the introduction of one or more hypothetical assumptions. That is, the introduction of a condition that did not exist as of the valuation date, but that is to be incorporated into the analytical process that is used for the determination of value.

You need to be careful to make sure that the management assumptions are forecasts, rather than projections. Sometimes projections can happen inadvertently. If a valuation is based on a hypothetical assumption, then the basis of the determination of value is dramatically different and requires further analytical work, since projections typically relate to matters that do not exist as of the selected valuation date but which are conditional on the occurrence or realization of the stated hypotheticals.

For example, keep in mind that Uniform Standards of Professional Appraisal Practice (USPAP) Standards Rule 9–2 (g) requires identification of any hypothetical conditions that are assumed, and it further states that a hypothetical condition may be used in an assignment only if:

- Use of the hypothetical condition is clearly required for a legal purpose, for purposes of reasonable analysis, or for purposes of comparison;
- Use of a hypothetical condition results in a credible analysis; and
- The appraiser complies with the disclosure requirements set forth in USPAP for hypothetical conditions.

Therefore, you should carefully monitor these differences. A common-sense approach to detect the use of a hypothetical assumption in a forecast is to look for any what-if or conditional statements that are presented. In some instances, the unknowing use of hypotheticals in an appraisal assignment may result in a lack of relevance to the actual facts and circumstances of the assignment; therefore, the opinion may not be found to be credible.

 ## REPORTING YOUR OPINED RESULTS

Keeping in mind that the purpose of a business valuation report should be to communicate the results of the foundational analysis that is performed, supporting the opinion offered, business appraisal standards universally require that a valuation analyst develop a clear and unequivocal basis for the opinion of value.

Let's look at a few report writing do's and don'ts to consider.

- **Reserve the use of the term *opinion* for the actual opinion.** Do a word search to identify where, throughout the report, you have used the word *opinion*. Remember that according to the foundational framework we established with the Credibility Pyramid, the opinion rests at the very top of the foundational hierarchy. Therefore, you should consider not using the term *opinion* until you are ready to state it. In many reports, you might notice that an opining individual uses the term *opinion* so often, you may wonder, How many opinions does he or she have? Instead, consider using other phrases, such as "in summation," "in summary," and similar terminology in all of the sections of your report that precede the actual opining paragraph and thus reserve the use of the term *opinion* to the expression of the actual opined results.

- **Before you write down any opinion language, you should consider revisiting the objectives that you set out to accomplish.** Your opinion should address the goals, purposes, and objectives that you stated. The opinion language should have a direct nexus to the analysis that is performed.

  When you read the opinion language, you should make sure that it is supported by all of the work you performed. For example, you should be ready to quickly respond to the question: What is the basis of your opinion?

  Consider the appropriateness of stating your opinion in terms of a range. This can be done in various ways. For example, the opinion itself may be stated in the form of an opined range, or you may establish a range of probable values or results as part of your reasonableness tests, and then you could choose a point within that range as the opined amount.

  If appropriate, the author recommends the latter, as it may serve two important purposes:

  1. It provides a range for a decision maker to consider.
  2. It points the decision maker to a specific data point within that range that, given the considered facts and circumstances, the opining individual has chosen.

▪ **Avoid analytical gaps.** Make sure that all aspects of your report clearly state, define, and discuss those foundational facts, analyses, inferences, or summations that form the bases for your opinion. This should help you avoid analytical gaps.

▪ **Conclusions and summations**. Make sure that each major section of your report concludes with a summary stating your findings. Remember, do not use the term *opinion* as you conclude each section.

Your conclusions and summations need to create a logical nexus to the next logical part of your analysis. For example, in the determination of value, by the time you apply the selected methodologies to your analysis, your *conclusions should cover several relevant matters* that affect the application of your methodologies, as of the valuation date, including:

▪ A supported growth rate for your subject that considers then-existing economic and industry conditions.

▪ Your subject's comparative performance versus its industry peers'.

▪ Identified risks, deficiencies, or issues then existing.

▪ An understanding of competitive forces in the marketplace affecting your subject.

▪ A forward-looking understanding of the financial resources available to your subject, including its cash flow–generating capacity, value drivers, and asset composition.

Make sure that you can replicate all information presented in your report.

Be sure to stay within your field of expertise. Do not opine on matters beyond your field of expertise.

Consider the appropriateness of formulating your opinion in terms of a range. This can be done in different ways. For example, the opinion itself may be stated in the form of an opined range, or you may establish a range of probable values or results as part of your reasonableness tests, and then you could choose a point within that range as the opined amount.

If appropriate, the author recommends the latter, as it may serve two important purposes:

1. It provides a range for a decision maker to consider.
2. It points the decision maker to a specific data point within that range, which, given the considered facts and circumstances, the opining individual has chosen as a result of the work performed.

CONCLUSION

When all is said and done, hopefully you can sit back and read your opinion and feel comfortable with it. For example:

> In the opinion of the valuation analyst, using the generally accepted valuation methods and *subject to the limiting conditions and assumptions incorporated in this report,* the fair market value of the subject interest, comprising a single block of Two Thousand Four Hundred and Fifty Common Shares, representing 49 percent of the no par value, common stock, the only class of stock authorized, issued and outstanding, on a not freely marketable minority basis of XYZ Inc., as of December 31, 2010, is best expressed as $1,850,000.

Note the precise definition of the subject interest used, defining the level of value, as well as the ownership characteristics of the interest valued. You should have used the same description of the subject interest in your engagement memorandum.

In this chapter, we have reviewed important elements of your analysis that affect the credibility of your proffered results, touching on the sufficiency and overall reasonableness of your findings. We have also discussed the development of several of the credibility attributes, such as transparence, replication, and relevance.

Chapter 7 discusses reasonableness tests and related procedures.

 ## NOTES

1. Rev. Rul. 59–60, 1959-1 CB 237—IRC Sec. 2031.
2. Institute of Business Appraisers, Plantation, Florida. Continuing Education Course #1007, "Developing and Defending Fractional Interest Valuation Premiums and Discounts."
3. *IRS Valuation Guide for Income, Estate and Gift Taxes* (Commerce Clearing House, 1994), p. 9-3.
4. Shannon P. Pratt, Robert F. Reilly, and Robert P. Schweihs, *Valuing a Business: The Analysis and Appraisal of Closely Held Companies*, 4th ed. (New York: McGraw-Hill Companies, 2000), p. 393.
5. *Guide to Business Valuations*, vol. 2 (Practitioners Publishing Corporation, 2012), para. 803.40.
6. Dennis Bingham, "An Analysis of Discount for Lack of Marketability Models and Studies," *Business Appraisal Practice* (Institute of Business Appraisers: Plantation, FL, 2011.)

7. Institute of Business Appraisers, Plantation, Florida. Continuing Education Course #1007, "Developing and Defending Fractional Interest Valuation Premiums and Discounts."

8. Johnson Study, Bruce Johnson, "Quantitative Support for Lack of Marketability Discounts," Shannon Pratt's Business Valuation Library, October 2001.

9. The appraiser tested this observation by reference to the industry risk premia index, published by Ibbotson and Associates.

10. Gilbert E. Mathews, "Cap x = Depreciation Is an Unrealistic Assumption for Most Terminal Values; Frequent Error Causes Observation," *Business Valuation Resources*, http://bvlibrary.com, March 2002.

7

Reasonableness Tests

A S YOU NEAR THE COMPLETION of an engagement, the Credibility Pyramid requires that you formulate a set of procedures that are intended to be supportive and probative of the opinion about to be proffered as a result of your analytical process. I refer to those procedures as "reasonableness tests," which I like to define as "analytical procedures applied to the opined results with the objective of establishing a commonsense and logical inference, void of speculation, on which to reach a supportive and probative *assertion* of the proffered results."

For educational purposes, I find it useful to look to the following judicial guidance on what constitutes "reasonableness":

> Articulating precisely what "reasonable suspicion" and "probable cause" mean is not possible. They are commonsense, nontechnical conceptions that deal with the factual and practical considerations of everyday life on which reasonable and prudent men, not legal technicians[,] act. As such, the standards are not really, or even usefully, reduced to a neat set of legal rules. We have described reasonable suspicion simply as a particularized and objective basis for suspecting the person stopped of criminal activity, and probable cause to search as

existing where the known facts and circumstances are sufficient to warrant a man of reasonable prudence in the belief that contraband or evidence of a crime will be found. We have cautioned that these two legal principles are not "finely-tuned standards" comparable to the standards of proof beyond a reasonable doubt or of proof by a preponderance of the evidence.

They are instead fluid concepts that take their substantive content from the particular contexts in which the standards are being assessed. The principal components of a determination of reasonable suspicion or probable cause will be the events which occurred leading up to the stop or search, and then the decision whether these historical facts, viewed from the standpoint of an objectively reasonable police officer[,] amount to reasonable suspicion or to probable cause.[1]

In light of the above guidance, it logically follows that reasonableness tests (RTs) should be considered in terms of the applicable framework on which the opinion is to be proffered. For example, in the determination of value, the framework is defined in terms of the agreed upon standard of value and its related premise. Consequently, it would be generally accepted that a "reasonable" conclusion under a hypothetical fair market value standard would not comport to a "reasonable" conclusion under a fair value or some other standard of value.

DETERMINING REASONABLENESS

Typically, reasonableness tests will fall into two categories:

1. **Those applied to specific elements of an analytical process.** For example, during the derivation of a cost of capital metric for a given subject, you may test the reasonableness of your results by trying to allocate the derived cost of capital to the asset base, in terms of the estimated required rates of returns applicable to each, in order to determine whether the derived composite result leads to a "reasonable" calculation.

2. **Those applied to the overall opined result.** For example, you may use an internal rate of return analysis to test the reasonableness of the opined value by relating it to the calculated benefit stream that is attributed

to that subject interest. An overall reasonableness test conclusion may require that you go back and reconsider the result of your analytical process; for example, the results of your overall reasonableness test may point to:

a. A lack of sufficient data and/or a need to expand your analytical scope.
b. Inadequate assumptions.
c. Selected methodology lacking relevancy to the objectives of the engagement.

Always keep in mind that the reasonableness test methodology that is used must be relevant with respect to the opined results and assessed and just as reliably applied as any primary methodology. All data sources that are used should be clearly documented. RTs should also incorporate the following components:

- Reasonableness tests must be void of any analytical gaps.
- Reasonableness tests' conclusions should be reconciled to the opined results.
- A reasonableness test should conclude with a clear and concise statement.
- Whenever possible, the selected range and/or data used should be based on observable market value parameters, subject to estimation:

The district court stated that plaintiffs' approach has two flaws, each fatal: first, because Sentinel did not own 100% of Falcon, it is impossible to derive the value of the whole firm from the amount paid for its holdings; second, the amount that Sentinel was paid depended on how much Khan and Falcon could borrow rather than Falcon's true value. Neither of these propositions is sound; indeed, each supposes that there is some measure of "true" value that differs from what a willing buyer will pay a willing seller in an arms'-length transaction. Yet that is the gold standard of valuation; other measures are approximations. The value of a thing is what people will pay. The judiciary should not reject actual transactions prices when they are available.[2]

In the same fashion that your analytical process should have endeavored to embrace those unique facts and circumstances of the engagement, any reasonableness test should be similarly conceived:

State-Boston's expert, Candace Preston, testified that the entire 38 percent decrease in Bancorp's stock price on October 26, 2007, resulted from the materialization of that risk. As described in part II, supra, Preston attempted to isolate the effect of company-specific factors from the effect of general market trends by comparing the change in the Bancorp's stock price to the change in the S&P 500. She also attempted to separate the effect of company-specific factors from industry-wide trends by comparing Bancorp stock to the NASDAQ Bank Index, an index of the stock prices of hundreds of banks and bank holding companies traded on the NASDAQ.

Preston failed, however, to account for the effects of the collapse of the Florida real estate market. The NASDAQ Bank Index may be well suited to capture the effects of national trends in the banking industry, such as the broader national financial crisis that reached its nadir in 2008. But in 2007, Florida, having benefitted more than most states from the real estate boom of the previous years, was hit harder than most by the ensuing bust. And Florida['s] 28 financial institutions, as Preston admitted on cross-examination, made up only a small percentage of the NASDAQ Bank Index. That index, therefore, would be inappropriate for the task of filtering out the effects of industry-wide factors that might affect the stock price of a bank, or of the holding company of a bank, whose assets were concentrated in loans tied to Florida real estate in 2007. BankAtlantic is just such a bank. As Bancorp acknowledged in several public SEC filings during the class period, BankAtlantic's assets were concentrated in loans tied to Florida real estate. As a result, BankAtlantic and Bancorp were particularly susceptible to any deterioration in the Florida real estate market, in addition to any national developments.[3]

Ultimately, the suitability of the procedures and methodologies to be used when conducting reasonableness tests rests on the sober exercise of informed professional judgment on the side of the opining individual.

Any number of factors may be taken into account in deciding whether there is reasonable suspicion to stop a car in the border area. Officers may consider the characteristics of the area in which they encounter a vehicle. Its proximity to the border, the usual patterns of traffic on the particular road, and previous experience with alien traffic are all relevant. They also may consider information about recent illegal border crossings in the area. The driver's behavior may be relevant, as erratic driving or obvious attempts to evade officers can support a reasonable suspicion. Aspects of the vehicle itself may justify suspicion. For instance, officers say that certain station wagons, with large compartments for fold-down seats or spare tires are frequently used for transporting concealed aliens. The vehicle may appear to be heavily loaded, it may have an extraordinary number of passengers, or the officers may observe persons trying to hide.[4]

Whenever formulating a set of reasonableness tests, always keep in mind that an opining individual should demonstrate that the reasonableness test conclusions are the results of commonsense and logical inferences *independently* derived from the reasonableness test data analyzed and applied to the engagement. With that thought in mind, I direct your attention to Revenue Ruling 59–60, which states (emphasis added):

> A determination of fair market value, being a question of fact, will depend upon the circumstances in each case. No formula can be devised that will be generally applicable to the multitude of different valuation issues arising in estate and gift tax cases. Often, an appraiser will find wide differences of opinion as to the fair market value of a particular stock. In resolving such differences, he should maintain a reasonable attitude in recognition of the fact that valuation is not an exact science. A sound valuation will be based upon all the relevant facts, but the elements of *common sense, informed judgment and reasonableness* must enter into the process of weighing those facts and determining their aggregate significance.

Furthermore, keep in mind that the reasonableness test results themselves can be subjected to further statistical analysis, regression techniques, and sensitivity analysis, as well as any other analytical techniques.

In conclusion, the information used in performing a reasonableness test must not be speculative and should always be as relevant to the facts and circumstances of the engagement as the information used in your primary analytical process. Whenever feasible, try to use data and methods that are market based and independent, to the extent possible, of the analytical process already undertaken. Reasonableness should be established on the basis of what a similarly situated, prudent entity/individual acting in good faith would consider reasonable, given the nature and purpose of the engagement. Industry norms and expectations may be taken into account when deriving a reasonableness test. In the following pages, you will find three examples of reasonableness tests applied to the determination of value.

EXAMPLE 1: DERIVED ESTIMATE OF VALUE

A reasonableness test of the derived estimate of value can also be useful in gaining an understanding of the thought process that both a hypothetical buyer and a hypothetical seller under the fair market value standard would undergo in assessing the appropriateness of a derived value estimate.

The following methodologies were used as part of the foundational support for the derived estimate of value:

- South Florida freight-forwarding industry rules of thumb.
- The internal rate of return.

Application of Industry Rules of Thumb

Rules of thumb are industry benchmarks that are usually stated in ranges, such as one to five times earnings before interest and taxes (EBIT). They can vary greatly within the same industry depending on geographic, industry subsectors, and other factors. Rules of thumb ignore the purpose of the valuation and standards of value considerations, as well as the unique factors affecting the subject, such as risk, industry and economic factors, profitability (that is, nature and quality of earnings), growth rates, capital structure, liquidity, and other relevant factors that are generally considered by appraisers when preparing a comprehensive valuation. Finally, Revenue Ruling 59–60 concisely states the limitations of rules of thumb: "No formula can be devised that will be generally applicable to the multitude of different valuation issues."

Rules of thumb can be useful in assessing derived valuation results; however, a user of rules of thumb must be aware that as discussed previously, rules of thumb should not be used exclusively. Considering the above limitations and as part of the reasonableness test for the engagement, I compared South Florida's freight-forwarding rules of thumb to the results obtained. To do so, I consulted with local business brokers, and I was able to determine that a typical freight-forwarding establishment in the South Florida area sells for approximately 2.5 to 3.5 times the two most recent years' owners' discretionary cash flow before interest and taxes, excluding the effects of any real estate or nonoperating assets. I found those findings supportive of results derived under the income approach valuation methodology, where a valuation multiple of 2.42 was applied to the calculated benefit stream, averaged discretionary earnings, under the multiple of discretionary earnings method.

The Internal Rate of Return

Since the internal rate of return (IRR) provides a simple hurdle rate for investment decision making, I found it particularly useful for this portion of the reasonableness test procedures. Ideally, the internal rate of return can be expected to exceed the firm's cost of capital, its discount rate. Therefore, investors use the IRR in determining the reasonableness of a particular investment (that is, a breakeven rate of return, indicating when the value of the cash outflow equals the value of cash inflow). Although IRR does not measure the absolute size of an investment or its return, it is a suitable tool for a reasonableness test.

A hypothetical buyer and a hypothetical seller would make a similar analysis in reaching a decision as to whether to enter into a fair market value transaction at the derived estimate of value. The use of this methodology is considered generally acceptable by valuation analysts in arriving at a reasonableness test conclusion.

In order to use the IRR as threshold criteria, I estimated a proxy for the subject's cost of capital. Although there are various methods suitable for the calculation of a firm's estimated cost of capital, for the purpose of the reasonableness test, the appraiser relied on the market data provided by the Cost of Capital Center, *2003 Yearbook*, published by Ibbotson and Associates. A risk factor for incremental risk was added to account for company-specific unsystematic risk factors other than size, more specifically:

Industry cost of equity capital for SIC Code 4731	
Based on three-stage discounted cash flows	11.80 percent
Add: specific company risk premium for factors	
(other than size) of subject company	11.00 percent
Equals: proxy for net cash flow discount rate	<u>23.00</u> percent (rounded)

The considerations, which lead to the selection of the incremental return for factors other than size, are explained in Exhibit 7.1. Seven factors were

Company Characteristic Assessed by Appraiser	Elements Considered	Discussed in This Report in Section
1. Access to Additional Capital	Limited relationships with financial institutions.	4.1
2. Financial Risk	Inadequate liquidity, as evidenced by below-industry working capital levels.	4.1
3. Product Lines	Product line diversification vs. competitors'. Product lines were assessed as competitive.	3.6
4. Diversification	Customer dispersion versus concentrations. As of the valuation date, no concentrations were found.	3.4
5. Technology Base	While the subject has indicated a commitment to keep up technologically, past financial practices have limited its ability to devote additional capital to develop its technology base.	3.15
6. Industry & Regulatory Risk	Effect of statutory customs, homeland security regulation, and related matters are acting as barriers to new industry entrants and making it difficult for customers to do without the subject's services.	2.35
7. Management Depth	Management depth was considered inadequate.	3.3
Total Subjective Company Risk Premium Assigned for Factors Other Than Size of Subject (1)		11%

EXHIBIT 7.1 Risk Premium Assessed by the Valuation Analyst

considered relevant in determining the subjective incremental company-specific risk premium. These factors may vary from company to company, among industries, and over time with the same company. The objective was to assess the company-specific risk drivers, based on the detailed industry and financial analysis that was performed, in order to estimate any additional incremental rate of return that a hypothetical buyer would require to offset any assessed added risk drivers specific to the company. In contrast to the industry-derived (and empirically developed) cost of equity capital data obtained from Ibbotson's Cost of Capital Center for SIC Code 4731, there is no objective or empirical basis for arriving at the relative weights given by the appraiser to the enumerated company-specific risk factors. They are presented as an aid to the reader in explaining the analyst's thought process in the application of informed judgment regarding the risk premium assessed.

Test Conclusion

Therefore, a specific company risk premium for unsystematic factors other than the size of 11 percent was applied. The Ibbotson's cost of equity capital is intended to be applied to net cash flow to equity holders. For the purpose of this analysis, the appraiser postulated that the market rate derived from Ibbotson's cost of equity capital data for SIC Code 4731 would be appropriate to this reasonableness test methodology.

The forecasted cash flow indicates an approximate internal rate of return of 21.8 percent (rounded), compared to the subject's proxy for its estimated cost of capital of 23 percent, which is in line with empirical cost of capital data for small businesses.[5]

Therefore, these results, calculated on the basis of the out-of-pocket assumed amount invested of $840,000 and the estimated future seller's discretionary cash flow determined on the basis of the forecasted annual industry growth in gross revenues of 7.4 percent, resulting in a forecasted 3 percent increase in the projected seller's discretionary cash flow, would tend to indicate a favorable decision.

EXAMPLE 2: GUIDELINE COMPANY METHOD

As part of the appraiser's consideration of the market approach, a search for comparable guideline companies was conducted. In applying the guideline company method as a reasonableness test, an appraiser selects an appropriate value multiple from the selected set of guideline companies. The multiple may be adjusted for the unique aspects of the company being valued in comparison to the guideline company. This multiple is then applied to the subject to arrive at an estimate of value for the appropriate ownership interest. Finally, any applicable premiums and/or discounts would be used.

The conceptual framework underlying the "guideline" company method is that the prices of publicly traded stocks in the same or similar industries provide objective evidence as to values at which investors are willing to buy and sell interests in similar companies in that industry. The guideline company method compares the subject to comparable individual guideline companies used as a proxy for the marketplace for similar interest. To be an equally desirable substitute for the subject closely held businesses, the guideline business must be both similar and relevant:[6]

- *Similar* refers to the nature of the business being appraised. It encompasses such business attributes as
  - Business size
  - Markets served
  - Depth of management

- Information processing systems
- Level of technology utilization
- Probable future earnings growth, and so on
- *Relevant* refers to the desires and expectations of the probable "willing buyer" or investor. This includes
  - Risk tolerance (degree of risk assumed)
  - Liquidity of investment
  - Degree of management involvement
  - Probable holding period, and so on

Therefore, in the appraisal of closely held interests, an appraiser must establish that the above "similar" and "relevant" criteria can be met before publicly traded guideline companies can be effectively used as market proxies in the valuation of closely held business interests.

Selection of the "Guideline" Company Group

A search of SIC Code 3728 in the EDGAR website and SIC Code 5088 in the Ibbotson's website under the category "industry analysis" yielded a combined group of seven possible guideline companies.[7] SIC Code 3728 consists primarily of aircraft parts manufacturing concerns, rather than distributorships; it was also reviewed because the EDGAR database did not have a listing for SIC Code 5088. Of the seven companies identified, one was in bankruptcy, another was a subsidiary, and a third did not file its annual financial information with the Securities and Exchange Commission; therefore, no data was available for it as of December 31, 2003. Two of the remaining four guideline companies had fiscal years ending in May and June, due to different operating cycles and product lines than the subject, thus making comparisons with the subject less relevant.

The aviation industry experts who were consulted (see Section 1.8) had suggested that public company number three was the best market proxy available. On further analysis, I concluded with these experts that company number three was indeed the best market proxy available for purposes of our analysis, because

- The selected guideline company's trade level (the company is an independent distributor) is similar to the subject's.
- The product line of the selected guideline company is similar to that of the subject.
- The guideline company's primary clientele (commercial airlines) is similar to the subject's.

The guideline company method was used only as a reasonableness test to value because of the restricted sample size, consisting of only one guideline company, the application of a revenue multiple in the methodology, and the fact that the selected guideline company was so much larger than the subject.

Normalized Adjustments to the Guideline Company Financial Information

Because a price-to-sales multiple was selected, normalized adjustments to the operating results of the subject and guideline companies, while considered, were not found to be necessary.

Selection of a Market Multiple

I selected the price-to-sales multiple of the guideline company as of December 31, 2003. The price-to-sales ratio is suitable when used as a reasonableness test on an equity value that has been determined by using a multiple period discounting method. I used the price-to-sales multiple of the selected guideline company, rather than the group, as the best market proxy, because only company number three's operating characteristics were found to be substantially similar, as indicated by similar gross profit and pretax margins. In summary, the appraiser concluded that the application of the price-to-sales multiple was viable, because under the facts and circumstances of this appraisal, it is reasonable to conclude that a given quantity of revenues should be able to produce a similar operating margin.

Calculation of Estimated Value: Guideline Company Method—a Market Approach

The subject company's gross sales for the year 2003 were selected as the most likely proxy indicator of the future revenue performance of the company. Then I applied the price-to-sales market multiple of the guideline company as of December 31, 2003, to the gross sales. In addition, the level of value derived under the guideline company method represents a marketable as if freely traded minority value as a result of the application of a market multiple derived from investments in which investors receive, in addition to a market rate of return, the liquidity of a freely and actively traded security. Because the purpose of the valuation is to arrive at a not freely marketable minority value, a discount for lack of marketability was deemed appropriate, as the subject's equity interest does not possess this degree of marketability. The calculation of estimated value under the guideline company method is as follows:

Reported year 2003 gross sales of subject	$14,578,400
Price-to-sales market multiple of the selected guideline company	.28
Indication of estimated value under the guideline company method marketable minority basis	$4,081,952
Divide by the number of total shares	5,000
Fair market value per share on a marketable basis	816
Less: discount for lack of marketability	237 (rounded)
Fair market value per share on a not freely marketable minority basis	579
Times: number of minority shares representing the percentage of interest valued (39% of 5,000)	1,950
Indication of estimated fair market value of one thousand nine hundred and fifty common shares, as a single block, representing 39 percent of the shares authorized, issued and outstanding, on a not freely marketable minority basis	$1,100,000 (rounded)

The guideline company method indicated a reasonableness test value of $1,100,000 (rounded) for a single block of 1,950 common shares on a not freely marketable minority basis, after the application of a 29 percent discount for lack of marketability. The discount for lack of marketability was derived on the basis of the analysis performed in Section xx of this report. A discount for lack of control was not considered necessary, because it is already implicit in the market-derived minority data used in this methodology.

There are valuation analysts who question the validity of the conceptual framework underlying the guideline company methodology when applied to the valuation of a closely held business interest, on the grounds that the value drivers at work in the public markets are quite different from the motivations of buyers and sellers of interests in closely held businesses. Namely, one of these arguments is based primarily on size: as a business entity becomes larger in size, the motivations of investors, management, and stockholders tend to differ greatly. Empirical support for price-earnings ratio differences, due to company size, can be found in an independent published study conducted by Jerry O. Peters.[8]

In this study, Peters compiled median public company price earnings ratios by total company market value for both control transactions (Mergerstat annually 1985–1994) and public market transactions (Disclosure II

EXHIBIT 7.2 Four Guideline Companies

Symbol	Company	Exchange	Workforce	Annual Sales (millions)	5-Year Average Pretax Profit Margin	Debt-to-Equity Ratio	Price-to-Sales Multiple	Historical Sales Growth (%)	Market Cap (millions)
FAVS	First Aviation Services	NASDAQ	183	105	.7	.30	.33	-2%	30M
FA	The Fairchild Corporation	NYSE	5,500	630	2.3	1.30	.25	-10%	50M
AVL	Aviall, Inc.	NYSE	820	506	4.3	.46	.28	15%	150M
AIR	AAR Corporation	NYSE	2,500	874	5.1	.53	.43	-3%	240M

database monthly January 1992–April 1995). The results were remarkably similar between control and minority transactions, with both selling at slightly greater than a 25 percent price earnings discount for companies with a total market value under $25 million market capitalization, as compared with companies with total market capitalization of more than $100 million.

The general relationship was quite consistent over time, holding up for all 10 of the years in the control transaction study and all 40 of the months in the minority transaction study.

In an effort to account for these potential size differences, the derived estimate of value obtained under the application of the guideline company method, $1,100,000, when considered in light of the Jerry Peters study findings, would yield an adjusted approximate value of $825,000 (75 percent of $1,100,000).

Test Conclusion

The resulting values derived from the guideline company method yielded an indication of estimated fair market value of one thousand nine hundred and fifty common shares, as a single block, representing 39 percent of the shares authorized, issued, and outstanding, on a not freely marketable minority basis in the amount of $1,100,000, which, when adjusted for potential size differences, indicated a possible range between $825,000 and 1,100,000 for the subject interest (rounded). This range was found to be reasonable and supportive of the opined amount.

 ## EXAMPLE 3: USE OF MARKET MULTIPLES

Reasonableness tests are procedures used by business appraisers to test the reasonableness of derived estimates of value. They can be useful in gaining an understanding of the thought process that both a hypothetical buyer and a hypothetical seller, under the fair market value standard, would undergo in assessing the derived fair market value estimate.

Application of Rules of Thumb

Valuation multiples vary substantially, due to factors such as size, geographic location, client loyalty, and capital structure. In addition, valuation multiples can be expected to be lower in law firms, due to the nature of the goodwill, because value in a law firm is normally found to be measured to a greater extent in the lawyer equity holder personal attributes, more so than to those institutional intangible enterprise-related value drivers. However, based on the figures used in accounting and medicine, it would appear that the multiplier for the rule-of-thumb method should be in the same range for law practices that are subject to the previous considerations. Finally, it should be noted that most rules of thumb derived from the sale of law practices are relatively recent.[9]

Working with these limitations, and as part of the reasonableness check I performed, I compared the rules of thumb to the results obtained. While doing so, I found that according to the *Lawyer's Guide to Buying, Selling, Merging and Closing a Law Practice*, revenue multiples for law firms can fall in a likely range of .5 to 1.50 of fees. *The 2008 Business Reference Guide* reports multiples of .4 to 1 of annual revenues.[10] I also referred to the price-to-sales multiple of the only public company involved in this sector, but the transactions were found to be synergistic. Therefore, the price-to-sales multiple of this public company, although derived from marketable transactions, could not be relied on to yield credible benchmarks for the purpose of performing a reasonableness test.

Test Conclusion

The resulting values derived from the single-period capitalization method yielded price-to-fees multiples of approximately 35 percent, versus the rules of thumb of 40–50 percent, discussed earlier.

These differences were found to be reasonable in light of the economic and industry downturns and the additional incremental risks of the subject firm, as determined in the cost of capital derivation.

EXAMPLE 4: FEDERAL TAX COMPLIANCE

You must be able to prove that the pay is reasonable. Base this determination on the circumstances that exist when you contract for the services, not those that exist when the reasonableness is questioned. If the pay is excessive, the excess is disallowed for deduction.

For a comparative perspective, the following example, "Test 1: Reasonableness," is a reasonableness test sourced from Publication 535 (2011), *Business Expenses*, taken from the Internal Revenue Service at www.irs.gov/publications/p535/ch02.html.

Note how the reasonableness test presented here is structured as a fact-finding exercise, which, given the nature of the applicable framework and federal tax compliance, produces not an inference but more of a regulatory "more likely than not" certainty instead of the inferential premise that I previously proposed.

Factors to Consider

Determine the reasonableness of pay by the facts and circumstances. Generally, reasonable pay is the amount that like enterprises pay for the same or similar services. To determine whether pay is reasonable, also consider the following items and any other pertinent facts:

- The duties performed by the employee.
- The volume of business handled.
- The character and amount of responsibility.
- The complexities of your business.
- The amount of time required.
- The cost of living in the locality.
- The ability and achievements of the individual employee performing the service.
- The pay compared with the gross and net income of the business, as well as with distributions to shareholders if the business is a corporation.
- Your policy regarding pay for all of your employees.
- The history of pay for each employee.

 CONCLUSION

Yet regardless of the applicable framework, you need to keep in mind that RTs should be grounded in the presumption of what a reasonable and prudent person, exercising average care, skill, and judgment, would decide, given the particularly defined set of facts and circumstances that are applicable to that engagement. Under the determination of value, another element to consider is that a "reasonable and prudent person," as defined above, would also be considered to be a *hypothetical* individual acting under the assumptions and the premise of the stated standard of value.

Therefore, a reasonableness test, under the above-referenced definition, is not intended to be looked on as a replacement for a thorough analytical process, but rather as a reasonably prudent proposition in pursuit of an opined value. RTs should not be construed as implying a higher degree of confidence and/or reliability than what is already inherent in the analytical process previously undertaken or conceived as a replacement for the application of intellectual rigor during any step of the analytical process.

Industry norms, rules of thumb, market multiples, ratios, and the like, in and of themselves, should not be construed to be standalone reasonableness tests, although they may be used as part of, or as a component of a set of, reasonableness procedures.

In this chapter, you learned about reasonableness tests, which can be part of your efforts to establish reliability and relevance to the opined results. Keep in mind that reasonableness tests do not have to be standalone procedures that you perform as you ready to opine; they can also consist of procedures that you introduce throughout your analytical steps, applied on a basis consistent with the applicable standard of value.

Chapter 8 discusses enhancing the integrity of your opinion.

NOTES

1. *Ornelas v. United States*, 517 U.S., at 695–96 (citations omitted).
2. *Estate of Joe Lee Lott, Plaintiffs-Appellants. FALCON HOLDINGS, LLC, and ASLAM KHAN, Defendants-Appellees.* United States Court of Appeals for the Seventh Circuit (argued February 21, 2012; decided March 14, 2012).
3. *JOSEPH C. HUBBARD, et al., versus BANKATLANTIC BANCORP, INC., et al.,* United States Court of Appeals for the Eleventh Circuit (decided July 23, 2012).
4. *United States v. Brignoni-Ponce*, 422 U.S. 873, 883–84 (1975).
5. Raymond C. Miles, *Capitalization Rates in the Real World* (Plantation, FL: Institute of Business Appraisers, 1994).
6. Sourced from "A Market Data Tutorial," Institute of Business Appraisers, www .go-iba.org.
7. See http://valuation.ibbotson.com and www.sec.gov/info/edgar/siccodes.htm.
8. See Jerry O. Peters, "Adjusting Price/Earnings Ratios for Differences in Company Size—an Update," *Business Valuation Review*, September 1995, pp. 121–123.
9. K. William Gibson, ed., *Flying Solo: A Survival Guide for the Solo and Small Firm Lawyer*, 4th ed. (Chicago: American Bar Association, 2005).
10. Tom West, *2008 Business Reference Guide*, 18th ed. (Westford, MA: Business Brokerage Press, 2008), p. 402.

Enhancing the Integrity of Your Opinion

ONCE YOU HAVE REACHED THE top of your Credibility Pyramid, you need to take some time to reflect on your completed analytical process. At this time, there are nine factors that you should consider that can enhance the integrity of your opinion:

1. Understand the credibility threshold.
2. Understand the relevance and significance of the scope you have undertaken.
3. Understand the factual analytical responsibilities you have assumed.
4. Stay within your area of expertise—resist the temptation to cross over to an allied discipline. Keep the scope of your analytical process within your area of expertise.
5. Conduct your analysis within the parameters of economic reality relevant to the facts and circumstances of the engagement.
6. Maintain a high level of professional skepticism and engagement awareness.
7. Review your analytical process for relevance and typical common errors.
8. Unless you are licensed to practice law in your jurisdiction, resist the temptation to cite case law.
9. Be ready to respond to ethical challenges.

UNDERSTANDING THE CREDIBILITY THRESHOLD

Understanding the credibility threshold is an effective way to enhance the integrity of your opinion. In Chapter 2, among the credibility attributes, I introduced you to two aspects of credibility:

1. **Credibility is a threshold.** Once that threshold is crossed, adding more facts, additional analyses, and issues can cause paralysis by analysis in the stakeholders' minds, resulting in diminishing returns for the opining individual. Successful opining practitioners can detect these thresholds and prepare their opinions accordingly.
2. **Credibility does not exist in a vacuum.** It is supported by collaborating elements; see the eight attributes discussed earlier.

Now, let me take the previous concepts to the next level via the following diagram. As you can see, I am proposing that in fact there are two thresholds to be overcome: the initial threshold and the final threshold. The initial threshold is reached as a result of the conclusions and summations you present during the analytical process. As the users of your work product become familiar with your work, they may begin to attach credibility to it, provided that they can discern from your analytical process the credibility attributes that were discussed in Chapter 2 and thereafter.

As your stakeholders become familiar with your analytical process, and the basis of your opinion is supported via supporting evidence, especially if you have managed to step outside of the facts of the engagement and brought external real-world facts into your analysis, your stakeholders may then cross the final threshold and proceed to hold your opinion as "credible." See Exhibit 8.1.

I turn your attention to the concept of "cognitive dissonance" as an aid in understanding the credibility thresholds proposed here. The concept of cognitive dissonance holds that individuals react negatively to a set of facts or beliefs that are in contradiction to their already held set of personal beliefs. This psychological theory was initially developed by Leon Festinger, circa 1957, and subsequently developed by Festinger and others.[1]

The aspect of this concept that affects our analysis is that these researchers also found that cognitive dissonance impairs decision making. The researchers determined that when an individual experiences a state of cognitive dissonance, there are three likely outcomes:

1. A change in behavior.
2. Changing the perception of the conflicting cognition.
3. A need to add a new set of beliefs to justify any new behavior.

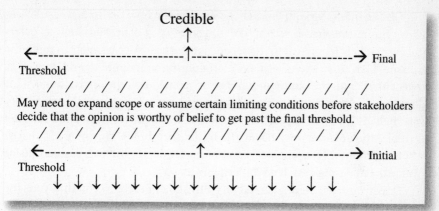

EXHIBIT 8.1 Credibility

On that basis, an opining individual should proceed under the premise that his or her opinion is likely to cause at least some degree of cognitive dissonance in the minds of the users of the opined work product, thus impeding the decision-making process that should follow. Moreover, If the opinion(s) causes too much cognitive dissonance, stakeholders may reject it and the opinion(s) may never make it past the initial threshold.

Therefore, the analytical process undertaken should readily present a way for stakeholders and decision makers to resolve this potentially negative reaction (that is, cognitive dissonance) as a means to reach the final threshold. If all, or a portion, of your analytical process leads to "paralysis by analysis" on the part of the stakeholder audience for your work product, it may be simply due to an information overload, rather than to any cognitive dissonance, caused perhaps by a perceived complexity of the subject matter.

Regardless of whether an opined result causes dissonance or not, also keep in mind that there are many instances when conclusions and summations will simply not rise past the first threshold, as the down arrows indicate—especially in instances where problems with the analysis performed are so profound that it would be impossible, even with an expansion of scope, for the opined results to be found credible by a stakeholder or a decision maker. For example, a lack of relevance, resulting from a failure to obtain factual information on which to make risk assessments; a failure to derive a reasonable growth rate; or hypothetical assumptions of conditions that did not exist as of the valuation date and whose forward-looking applications cannot be supported by the presence, as of the valuation date, of the necessary resources to carry them out or by misunderstanding the nature and history of the company's operations and/or past experiences.

On the other hand, there may be instances where an opined result rises above the initial threshold but, due to conditional concerns, such as external events, fails to make it to the second level, never surpassing the credibility threshold. In this type of situation, an opining individual would do well to reflect further on the matter at hand before concluding the analysis and, after doing so, decisively determine whether the conclusion meets the credibility threshold. If it fails to do so, then consider it below the threshold and thus not credible (the down arrows below the initial threshold). This may also occur when the results of reasonableness tests you conducted indicate results outside of an expected range, with no discernable reasons.

Once you have met the credibility threshold, I recommend that you stop your analytical process, because adding more data and analysis tends to offer diminishing returns and perhaps even makes it very difficult for your audience of intended users to comprehend the results presented, ultimately resulting in the aforementioned paralysis by analysis.

Remember, once you have met the credibility threshold of any given issue, it is then time to move on to the next part of the Credibility Pyramid that will need to be climbed.

UNDERSTANDING THE SCOPE UNDERTAKEN

Understanding the relevance and significance of the scope undertaken is another effective way to enhance the integrity of your opinion. The Credibility Pyramid established that your opinion should be based on an underlying foundational process. Such a process must be able to withstand the scrutiny and the analytical inquiries of those who are seeking to examine your opined results.

One of the easiest ways for an opining expert to compromise the integrity of his or her opinion is to end up with a poorly defined analytical scope. Sometimes, this may be happen due to pressures exerted on the opining expert. For example, during numerous depositions, you may be asked question after question having nothing to do with the matters on which you are opining; in such instances, you must be very cautious and consistently precise in your responses.

Remember that if you did not develop your analytical process in a rigorous enough fashion to deal with the question now before you, so that in fact you did not create a foundational basis for an opinion on the subject matter posed before you, you should not let yourself succumb to the pressure of an aggressive inquisition that is designed to force you to opine on any such unsupported issue.

During reviews of, or inquiries about, opined results, an opining individual may be placed under a great deal of pressure. For example, suppose that you are deposed, and opposing counsel questions the basis of your opinion by alleging that you should have considered certain aspects of an issue that you did not include in your analysis.

Moreover, you may be placed in a position that pressures you to opine on matters that are clearly outside the scope of the work you performed. The best response for you, under such circumstances, is to remain focused on the process that you initially defined. That is, recount your defined process, and indicate that because you have not applied that process to the new set of variables and the hypothetical information now presented before you, you are able to opine only on a hypothetical basis, which, by the way, has no relevance whatsoever to the facts and circumstances on which your opinion is in fact based.

In other words, an effective way to maintain the integrity of your opinion is to make sure that you opine only on matters that were specifically considered as part of the analytical process you have undertaken and that are supportive of the basis of your opined result(s).

Going outside the scope you have undertaken will compromise the integrity of your opinion and will cause you to lose credibility in other matters on which you may have otherwise correctly opined. An example of such an exchange, abstracted from a deposition testimony given by the author testifying as valuation analyst, follows:

Opposing Counsel: Mr. Analyst, you have testified in these proceedings that the value of the subject company is five million dollars, is that correct?

Mr. Analyst: No.

Opposing Counsel: Mr. Analyst, are you changing your opinion?

Mr. Analyst: No.

Opposing Counsel: I am confused, please explain.

Mr. Analyst: My testimony is that the fair market value of the subject interest, as outlined in my written report, is five million dollars as of December 31, 2011.

Opposing Counsel: Very well, then, Mr. Analyst, would you not agree that a reasonable valuation for this subject interest, as you defined it, as of December 31, 2000, would be five million dollars, considering the growth rates that you calculated as of December 31, 2011?

Mr. Analyst: No.

Opposing Counsel: Why not?

Mr. Analyst: Because I did not perform a valuation of the subject interest as of December 31, 2000. Therefore, I have no opinion on that matter.

Opposing Counsel: Mr. Analyst, isn't it true that the fair market value of the subject interest as of December 31, 2000, was overstated when that valuation was then performed?

Mr. Analyst: I have no opinion on the matter posed by your question. I did not perform a valuation of the subject interest as of December 31, 2000, nor did I perform a review of the valuation conclusion reached by analyst X as of December 31, 2000; therefore, I have not formulated an opinion on the question you are asking me.

Valuation analysts are tasked with the determination of value. Value is determined as of a specified date. A change in the valuation date calls for a new and different opinion.

UNDERSTANDING ANALYTICAL RESPONSIBILITIES AND THE IMPACT OF MATTER/CAUSE/EFFECT ANALYSIS

Some opining individuals take the position that client information received from a client retains its character, namely, that it remains as "management's" or as "client's" information. I strongly disagree with that position.

If you recall, the foundational nature of the Credibility Pyramid is based on the proposition that a basis must exist for any given opinion. Therefore, if you obtain any information, whether or not received from management or, for that matter, from any source, internal or external, once you proceed to consider that information and you decide to make it a basis of your opinion, then at that moment, I suggest that you have now embraced that information, and, consequently, it is now your information. In essence, you now "own it," and it is no longer just "management's information" or information provided by the client.

Therefore, an opining individual needs to be very clear when "anything" becomes a basis for a proffered opinion because then, at that point in time, that "thing" becomes the "property" of that opining individual. Therefore, you need to follow these four steps:

1. Identify the basis for your opinion—you should always consult with legal counsel on this matter, because there may be rules of civil procedure that may in fact require that such identification be included as part of your report.

2. Research and independently establish the relevance of any information before you incorporate it (that is, "embrace it") as part of your foundational work supporting your opinion (in other words, make it a part of your Credibility Pyramid).
3. Perform a matter/cause/effect analysis. In this type of critical thought process, you start by identifying the nature, characteristics, and attributes of a particular issue, fact, methodology, or procedure that you plan to introduce or consider part of your analytical process. Then you proceed by assessing the effect that the inclusion of that matter (the particular issue, fact, methodology, or procedure) causes via its inclusion in your analytical process, before you make a final determination as to whether to embrace the matter, in terms of the following parameters:
   a. Materiality.
   b. Consistency of treatment.
   c. The application of your informed judgment.
   d. Whether the matter meets the credibility attributes discussed in Chapter 2 (that is, relevance, reliability, replication, general acceptability, nonadvocacy, and so on).
4. Stay within your area of expertise—resist the temptation to cross over to an allied discipline.

To determine value, valuation analysts assess and calculate benefit streams on the basis of historical and prospective growth rates that the defined class of ownership is likely to derive. Typically, the determination of a set of growth rate assumptions is made on the basis of the known or knowable information as of a specified date. Therefore, you, as an opining individual, should always be mindful of attempts that are intended to corner you into rendering a new or second opinion on the basis of a growth rate assumption hypothetically derived on either a retroactive, prospective, or any other basis, other than the one adopted on the basis of your consideration of relevant facts and circumstances.

In a related allied discipline, forensic accounting, a forensic analyst may use techniques such as "but-for analysis" and "yardstick analysis" in order to estimate economic damages. All of these techniques may also involve a determination of an economic benefit stream that the alleged injured party could have enjoyed. When engaged to determine economic damages, valuation analysts look at the process as the impact of conditions that cause a reduction or an impairment of the realization of the identified benefit stream attributed to the alleged injured party. This definition implies that

- A calculation of the benefit stream be made.
- A determination be made as to whether the reduction or impairment of the benefit stream is permanent.

It is similarities such as the previous facts and circumstances that may tempt a valuation analyst to readily think of himself or herself as a suitable expert to determine economic damages, because, as one can see, the skill sets may appear to be quite similar. However, a valuation analyst who is engaged to perform a valuation analysis that leads to a conclusion of value should not opine on a lost profit determination issue, even if this is inherent in the facts and circumstances of a given case, *unless the valuation analyst has the proper training and qualifications and has proceeded in fact to expand the scope of the engagement to deal with the determination of economic damages.*

A similar situation arises when a valuation analyst, possessing no training as a reviewer, is tasked to review the value determination of another analyst. It is even more problematic if, in addition, the same valuation analyst is also tasked to proffer an opinion of value on the same subject interest that was reviewed. My advice in these types of situations is to select the role that you intend to play: valuation analyst or valuation reviewer. Stay away from any potentially incompatible situation that compromises any opinion to be proffered.

CONDUCT YOUR ANALYSIS WITHIN THE PARAMETERS OF THE ECONOMIC REALITY RELEVANT TO THE FACTS AND CIRCUMSTANCES

The following case points out the likely pitfalls that will be encountered when the economic reality that is relevant to the facts and circumstances of a case is ignored. This can quickly lead to a "push down" effect on credibility, as depicted in the credulity threshold graph (Exhibit 8.1) earlier in the chapter. It ultimately results in a total denial of credibility—that is, not just in regard to that one issue or premise, but the opined result (for example, the opinion of value, the opinion of economic damages, and so on) will be held as incredible.

Kohler generally used two types of projections to plan for its business. These projections were called the management plan and the operations plan, and each had different uses. The management plan was a set of achievable targets and reflected the realities of the business and management's best judgment of where the company would be. The management plan was given to outsiders intending to transact with Kohler, such as insurance companies and banks. Kohler also used the management plan internally for capital planning, acquisition planning, and tax planning. Management intended the management plan to be a good predictor of the company's performance and updated the management plan throughout the year to reflect Kohler's actual results. Kohler also developed an operations plan, which was a projection of what could theoretically be achieved in a perfect environment. The operations plan was built on the assumptions that each business unit would maximize its results and no contingencies or unforeseen events would occur. The operations plan was not generally updated throughout the year to incorporate new information or unforeseen events.

The management plan projected earnings for 1999 to be below those for 1998 and 1997, reflecting the difficulties in the international markets at the time and economists' predictions of either slow growth or a decline in the United States economy. Indeed, Herbert was aware of excesses creeping into the market and knew the company's international investments were not doing well.

Dr. Hakala (expert for the respondent) created two DCF models, one using revenues from the operations plan and one using revenues from the management plan. He weighted the results he derived from these two DCF models in a manner inconsistent with the reality of the business. He weighted the realistic management plan based model 20 percent and the more aspirational operations plan based model 80 percent because he thought the aspirational operations plan was a more likely scenario.[2]

MAINTAIN A HIGH LEVEL OF PROFESSIONAL SKEPTICISM AND ENGAGEMENT AWARENESS

Now and then, we should sit back and reflect from a skeptical perspective on things that we do routinely. As professionals, we are continually facing the challenge of achieving a level of general acceptability among valuation practitioners. Maintaining a degree of professional skepticism is a healthy endeavor and indeed, hopefully, conducive to productive intellectual discourse.

With these thoughts in mind, let me share with you some of my own skeptical thoughts while dealing with what I would call "valuation proxies" that I used in place of other procedures and methodologies, which may also lead to analytical gaps:

■ Consider instances where the argument is successfully articulated that a guideline company methodology lacks relevance to an engagement, and yet, in other sections of the same report, publicly derived market indices are used and applied to other selected procedures, such as in the derivation of cost of capital metrics and valuations adjustments, such as the discount for lack of control, discount for lack of marketability, or any other valuation adjustment where the data being used is in fact derived from public markets. For example, remember those IPO and restricted stock studies? The data came from public market sources, yet an analyst may have chosen to apply it to derive discounts for not freely marketable enterprises, previously assessed in the same report, as lacking the required attributes to qualify as suitable candidates for the application market approach methodologies, such as the guideline company method.

■ Development of discrete forecasts without considering effects of the inherent assumptions made elsewhere in the forecast on the resulting capital structure.

■ When justification of a purchase price is used as a reasonableness test when valuing minority interests, beware that in many instances the assumptions used may be attributed to a control position, and therefore not applicable to a minority level of value.

■ Normalizing adjustments that introduce synergies to a fair market valuation.

■ Using growth rates that ignore the stage of the industry and/or the available resources as of the valuation date.

■ Using assumptions that are not supported by the outlined facts in your report, such as instances when projections, rather than forecast assumptions, are incorporated into a valuation, which create hypothetical, "what-if" conditions that are not present on the valuation date.

■ Proffering inconsistent risk assessments without reconciling explanations. For example, deriving a low-cost capital metric (leading to a high value) while assessing a high discount for lack of marketability (leading to a low value) without a logical explanation.

■ High derived levels of discounts for lack of marketability when the financial analysis points to high liquidity and dividend capacity, with no further explanation or analysis presented to reconcile these issues.

- Ignoring the relevance of the marketplace in which the subject company operates, as well as the marketplace in which the subject interest may be ultimately liquidated, especially when there may be marked differences between each one.

- Different interpretations of the same concepts. For example, *fair market value*, as that term is defined for estate and gift tax purposes, is materially different from the interpretations of fair market value adopted by different jurisdictions. In some instances, jurisdictions that follow the fair market value standard may look to an investment value standard to rule on an opinion of value of an asset that lacks marketability but that nevertheless has value to a retaining spouse. Studying these California cases, *In Re: The Marriage of Cream* (1993) and *In Re: The Marriage of Hewitson* (1983), for example, and becoming familiar with the following different fair market value interpretations could be very helpful in assisting a valuation analyst to reasonably explain away such differences, when responding to conceptual foundational challenges to his or her opined result.

Revenue Ruling 59–60	Matrimonial Setting
Rev Ruling 59–60 fair market value standard: Hypothetical willing parties acting under no compulsion	Fair market value in a matrimonial setting: Husband and wife usually under some form of compulsion to dissolve their marital union.
Access to information	Scope limitations are common.
No synergies considered under fair market value	Synergistic traits of a retaining spouse may add to the value drivers.
Discounts contemplated under fair market value	Subject to jurisdictional requirements, discounts are not typically considered unless at the discretion of the matrimonial trier of fact under special circumstances.
Hypothetical sale, liquidity assumptions	Typically, no sale, limited liquidity available to settle the marital estate.

You should exercise the high level of professional skepticism that I alluded to earlier and ask yourself the question: Why am I using fair *market* value as a matrimonial standard of value? I would suggest to you as a possible response that you consider: *because, a matrimonial trier of fact may be looking to the marketplace, within the framework of fair market value, with an expectation of finding an equitable and unbiased approach that brings a sense of fairness to the proceedings, so that an equitable settlement of the marital estate may be reached.*

At all times, maintain a high level of engagement awareness; for example, as courts of equity, matrimonial tribunals are typically interested in achieving an equitable distribution of the marital estate. Your valuation opinion provides a marital currency that can be used by the trier of fact to achieve the otherwise impossible judicial task of effecting an equitable distribution.

Make sure that your foundational work anticipates the informational needs of your intended stakeholders. In most jurisdictions, ultimately, a trier of fact looks to the expert testimony of a valuator to aid him or her in reaching a decision.

REVIEW YOUR ANALYTICAL PROCESS FOR RELEVANCE AND TYPICAL COMMON ERRORS

You may wish to consider the qualitative checklists included in Chapter 4. In addition, you may also wish to refer to the checklist at the end of this chapter.

Things go wrong very quickly when a valuation analyst is unable to properly apply the relevant case law to his or her valuation methodology. It is imperative that the valuation practitioner possesses a thorough understanding of the relevant case law. A valuation analyst must acquire an in-depth understanding of fair market value as a standard of value and know Revenue Ruling 59–60.

In many jurisdictions, when references are made to fair market value, no discounts are contemplated unless specifically indicated, for example, due to a court-ordered sale. Courts sometimes use the term *goodwill* to refer to all of the intangible assets of an enterprise; however, in other instances, the term *goodwill* is defined as the excess of the value over the fair market value of tangible assets and identified intangible assets.

Although you may not use all three, be sure to *consider* all three approaches to value. Beware of methodologies relying on forward-looking assumptions that may lack relevance to the facts and circumstances existing as of the valuation date. When making normalization adjustments, be sure to relate the adjustments to local industry metrics, whenever possible.

When using the market approach, be sure to establish the comparability of your subject to the marketplace, that is, guideline companies may not be comparable to closely held entities.[3]

If you decide to use a national salary market survey, be sure to establish its relevance to local salary levels. For example, see *In re the Marriage of Rosen*

(2002), where the California Court of Appeals ruled that a *national* survey of lawyer compensation was not a proper basis for offering an opinion on average lawyer compensation in *Southern California*. Economic and industry analyses must be relevant at the local level, not just at the national level. Beware of industry and seasonal trends and practical considerations. Be mindful of jurisdictional requirements. For example, when valuing a professional practice in California, requirements regarding the excess earnings method call for a determination of "a practitioner's *average* annual net earnings (before income taxes) over a *period of years.*

Make sure that you have included a critical analysis of the attributes of the *benefit stream valued*, the degree of reliance that you placed in your valuation methodology, and any applicable limitations.

Some valuation analysts like to refer to *fair value* when discussing matrimonial standards of value, but be very careful. Remember that statutory fair value is defined by specific jurisdictional statues: *statutory fair value attempts to eliminate oppression or suppression; marital standards of value deal with division of the marital estate.*

As a valuation analyst, you must determine and define what is to be valued, such as the invested capital of the enterprise, the equity, the debt-free operating assets, and so on. In a marital valuation, you may also have to determine what property may constitute personal goodwill, versus enterprise goodwill, and whether that property exists at all. The fair market value standard applies to property to be valued and not to any property excluded from the valuation of matrimonial interest. This is a crucial task that cannot be underemphasized. This determination is made in light of the jurisdictional requirements, case law, and the facts and circumstances of the case and with the aid and assistance of legal counsel.

Unless you are licensed to practice law in your jurisdiction, resist the temptation to cite case law. There are many times when an opinion must, by necessity, be guided by a statute, an administrative rule, a regulation, or case law, and the natural tendency by an opining individual is to quote such statute, case law, or regulation. In some instances, statements are also proffered to the effect that the methodologies employed conform to that particular statute or case law.

How could such a practice impair the integrity of your opinion? There are several arguments for you to consider:

■ When you quote or refer to case law as a precedent or requirement for a methodology or position that you may have incorporated into the basis for your opinion, you are making the assertion that the facts and circumstances underpinning that case law are the same as, or at least substantially similar to, those attending facts and circumstances for the subject case before you for consideration.

▪ Yet as natural a process as that might appear to you, if you stop and think about what you have just done, you should readily come to the realization that in applying the facts and circumstances of a particular legal case to the facts and circumstances of an engagement, you have *derived a legal conclusion*.

▪ Needless to say, unless you are qualified to practice law in the respective jurisdiction, the unauthorized practice of law could easily impair the integrity of your opinion, as well as expose you, as an opining individual, to sanctions and possibly fines.

A natural inquiry on your part should be: How do you consider case law without deriving a legal conclusion? My suggestion to you is as follows:

▪ Read editorials and articles published in professional publications examining the issue, and quote the published articles, not the case law.

▪ Read the case law with the purpose of gaining an understanding of the explanations and the reasoning. To the extent deemed appropriate, adopt the reasoning presented in the case into your valuation methodologies.

▪ In many instances, you may be able to refer to the adopted procedure as a generally accepted valuation procedure, because other practitioners in your area may have already adopted the precedent, and it is being used by those practitioners when they regularly conduct engagements under similar facts and circumstances.

Recall the definition of generally accepted practices presented in Chapter 4: Generally accepted appraisal practices in the United States of America are those approaches, related methodologies, and procedures thereunder that have been peer reviewed and exposed to publication and that can be reasonably expected to be used by other practitioners who are regularly conducting engagements under similar facts and circumstances.

 ## BE READY TO RESPOND TO ETHICAL CHALLENGES

There may be occasions when you may be summoned to discuss or review opinions that compete with your own. Alternatively, in other situations, you may also be asked to offer a second opinion to one being proffered by a competing opining individual. In such instances,

- Be sure to have all of the necessary facts provided to you before offering any responses and consider refusing to perform cursory "reviews" of the work of others.
- Be sure to maintain a clear distinction in your mind between the role of an opining individual and the role of stakeholders. Remember, when acting in the capacity of an opining individual, you should not assume the role of a decision maker.
- Keep your opining analytical process separate from the decision-making process.
- Request access to the other individual whose work product is now presented to you.
- Be very cautious whenever you are discussing your opined result at the same time as a previously derived opined work product performed by someone else at a different date and perhaps for a different purpose.
- Request, whenever possible, a conference with the other opining individual. If a conference is not practical or possible, consider including such inability as a limiting condition to whatever opinion you do offer.
- Consider performing a side-by-side analysis of the competing work products and identifying the matters that cause the differences in opined results. Thereafter, perform an objective analysis of the identified matters that cause the differences between the two opined results.
- Remember that there may be several possible outcomes to any set of facts and circumstances. In fact, all of these differing outcomes may be correct. At that time, you should consider pointing out to the stakeholder or decision maker that any one of these opined results may be held as credible. In fact, you may then wish to plot these various competing opined results and/or establish a range of possibilities from such an analysis, for further consideration by the stakeholders.

 ## ENHANCING THE INTEGRITY OF YOUR OPINION WHEN AT TRIAL OR IN HEARINGS

In most instances, your trial testimony will encompass the following separate and distinct phases:

- Direct examination is conducted by retaining counsel and is designed to present the expert evidence to support the theory of the case.

- Cross examination immediately follows direct examination. Opposing counsel may read from the pretrial deposition given by the expert in a question-and-answer format. Broad discretion is typically given by the judge to opposing counsel in questioning the expert.
- Redirect examination immediately follows cross examination. This gives your attorney a second chance to address issues brought up during cross examination.
- Recross examination immediately follows redirect. It is limited to the issues questioned during redirect.
- You must have a detailed understanding of the valuation resources that you are relying on.
- You must understand the methods and procedures that are used. For example, if you are using Ibbotson (Morningstar) to derive a built-up rate, you need to read chapters 1–9 of the *Ibbotson SBBI Yearbook* in order to understand the methodology and procedures used to derive the incremental risk premia presented in your valuation report.
- Always give attribution to any sources used.
- Preferably use footnotes at the bottom of each page, rather than end notes as part of a bibliography in the back of a report.
- Pay particular attention to sources of information that were known or knowable as of the valuation date.
- Your valuation methodology must be relevant.
- Your valuation methodology must address the identified level of value of the engagement.
- Your valuation methodology needs to be reliably applied and must assist the trier of fact. Make sure that your valuation analysis and explanations address central points of contention.
- Use reliable valuation methodology, know your confidence levels, and use regression analysis whenever appropriate, in order to establish the predictability of the information that you are using.
- Avoid subjective opinions; instead, take great care to explain how your methodology was reliably applied to the facts and circumstances of the case.
- Explain how and when you used informed judgment.
- Keep your professional training and CPE relevant to the subject matters on which you opine. Your testimony must have a foundation that addresses the issues raised in the "theory of the case."
- Your foundation should be created by the methodology that you used,

- Consult with legal counsel *prior* to developing your opinion regarding any applicable case law.
- Be sure that your methodology embraces any contractual requirements or relevant case law issues.

At trial, during all phases—direct, cross, redirect, or recross—of your valuation testimony, you must:

- Be yourself.
- Be precise.
- Be coherent.
- Be relevant.
- Not come across as belligerent or defensive.
- Never talk down when discussing technical valuation issues. Don't act like a hired gun.
- Avoid talking to anyone while you wait to be called.
- Sit by yourself.
- Dress conservatively but in such a way as to set yourself apart from the attorneys.
- Act, appear, and sound like a valuation expert, but keep your comments simple and easy to understand—use analogies, but don't be colloquial.
- Always maintain eye contact, and let the other party finish before you proceed to respond.
- Never give a legal opinion or conclusion. For example, don't ever refer to other valuation analysts as negligent or having committed malpractice; those are opinions calling for a legal conclusion on your part.
- Be polite above all else.
- Respond only to a specific question.
- Not talk if there is no question before you.
- Always respond in terms of the specific facts and circumstances that you have considered.
- Respond in a hypothetical way to hypothetical questions.
- Alert legal counsel of issues that are likely to come up during cross examination that he or she needs to deal with in redirect.
- Not count on legal counsel to bail you out of an issue in redirect that you had difficulty with during cross examination.
- Withstand the pressure during the cross examination of your testimony; otherwise, the integrity of your testimony may fall apart, and the credibility

of your testimony, which was established during direct examination, may be seriously challenged.

- Always be attentive to the way procedures are carried out in the courtroom.
- Always be prepared to tell the truth—you must maintain your professionalism by always taking the high road.

ENHANCING THE INTEGRITY OF YOUR OPINION WHEN AT DEPOSITION

For your expert testimony at deposition, note the following:

- Depositions can be very intense.
- Make sure that you are represented by counsel during any deposition.
- Take your time when answering all questions.
- Always respond to a stated question; if no question is before you, don't talk.
- Depositions are designed to probe for weaknesses in the bases, methodology, and foundation on your which expert opinion relies, to use at trial.
- You must prepare for a deposition in a similar manner to the way you would prepare for trial.
- Make sure that your report is completed before you are deposed.
- Be mindful of the fact that you are creating a record of your testimony, which may be read at trial.
- Avoid slang and colloquial language, stay formal, and address all relevant points.
- Be clear and concise. Do not use gestures; they cannot be recorded by the court reporter.
- Bring all of the relevant work papers and related files.
- Discuss with retaining counsel what you are bringing to the deposition and the document request served to you.
- Be ready to discuss every word in your engagement memorandum.

CONCLUSION

This chapter offered practice tips, suggestions, and information on how to enhance the integrity of your opinion. As an opining expert, you must always stand ready to maintain and project a high level of independence, as well as be able to demonstrate that your opinion was derived with integrity. You should also stand ready to demonstrate with ease the high level of intellectual rigor that you as an opining expert brought to bear in the search for the truth. In doing so, you need to be aware that stakeholders may perceive you in unintended ways, which in their minds may diminish the integrity of your opinion.

In Chapter 9, I discuss methods for reviewing the work of others.

 NOTES

1. Leon Festinger, *A Theory of Cognitive Dissonance* (Stanford, CA: Stanford University Press, new impression edition, 1957).
2. See T. C. Memo. 2006-152 *UNITED STATES TAX COURT HERBERT V. KOHLER, JR., ET AL.,1 Petitioners v. COMMISSIONER OF INTERNAL REVENUE*, Respondent Docket Nos. 4621-03, 4622-03, 4646-03, 4649-03. Filed July 25, 2006. Consolidated Brief, p. 40.
3. See the California case *In Re: The Marriage of Hewitson* (1983).

CHAPTER NINE

Reviewing the Work of Others

W HENEVER YOU SET OUT TO review the work of another expert, a useful technique is to start out by posing the following question of that individual: *Did you do what you said you were going to do?*

A powerful approach to reviewing the work of another expert is to establish a clear definition of the original purpose that he or she intended to fulfill and then construct a review methodology designed to assess whether the methods and procedures that were undertaken accomplished that purpose—and thereby establish whether the opinion proffered can be worthy of belief.

A reviewer should also be credible in designing and executing a review engagement. Just as the reviewer is expected to determine the credibility of the person under review, the reviewer is also expected to be credible. From a quality review approach, the expressed objective of a business appraisal review is to determine that the approaches and methodologies used by [name of the appraiser] were relevant to the objectives and purpose(s), as stated in the appraisal report prepared by [name of the appraiser] and applied on a reliable basis that is consistent with generally accepted appraisal practices in the United States of America as of [date of the business appraisal report].

In that regard, the following are key areas to consider any time that you set out to review the work of another expert. A review is the act or process of developing and communicating an opinion about the quality of all or part of the work of another individual.

Within this framework, a reviewer needs to be able to

- Use methodologies to effectively review the work product of others.
- Identify and articulate components of a business appraisal report that
  - Require additional support
  - Are inherently inconsistent
  - Lack relevance to the purpose of the engagement
  - Have an impact on credibility

Typical situations where business appraisal reviews may be needed are as follows:

- Financial reporting
- Fairness opinions
- Tax matters involving income, gift, and estate tax filings
- Regulatory filings and fiduciary oversights: Department of Labor, employee stock ownership plans, bank trustees
- Litigation support services: court proceedings, arbitration, mediation
- Mergers and acquisitions
- Internal in-firm reviews
- Alternative dispute resolution:
  - Transactional attorneys might include a review opinion requirement as part of a buy-sell or other shareholder agreement when both sides bring appraisers to the process.
  - A review opinion might have value for minority stakeholders, individually or as a group, who have an interest in the outcome of a shareholder dispute with the larger stakeholder group(s).
- Any other situation where an independent opinion regarding the credibility of the work product of a business appraiser would be useful to third parties.

It is also good to note who is retaining you. A reviewer may be retained by a client, its legal counsel, a business appraiser, or any other party interested in the results of an appraisal.

REVIEW ENGAGEMENT PROCEDURES TO CONSIDER

Prior to commencing a business appraisal review engagement, a reviewer should reach a written agreement with his or her retaining entity. This agreement should include, but is not limited to, the nature; the scope; the limitations, if any; and the assumptions of the proposed business appraisal review engagement, if any. It should also identify the reviewer's retaining entity, any intended users, the intended use of the reviewer's opinion, and the purpose of the review assignment and should define the role of the reviewer in the engagement, either as a consultant or adviser or as an expert. The nature of a business appraisal review engagement may call for changes to your traditional business appraisal engagement memo formats. It is strongly suggested that you consult with your legal counsel before adopting any changes or engagement procedures for your practice.

The following topics are presented for educational purposes and should not be considered a substitute for a reader's review of the full text of any related legal documents with the aid and consultation of qualified legal counsel:

- Include the reporting and certification formats and language that you are planning to use.
- State that a business appraisal review opinion is not an opinion of value.
- Clearly indicate that your business appraisal review services terminate on the delivery of your business appraisal review report.
- Clearly indicate your role either as a reviewing expert or as a reviewing consultant.
- If you are planning to obtain a representation letter from the client on conclusion of your engagement, be sure to indicate so in your appraisal review engagement memorandum.
- Unless otherwise agreed on with your client, indicate that the scope of your business appraisal review services is to be determined solely on the basis of the procedures that you deemed necessary in order to express a business appraisal review opinion.

In the event that a retaining entity concurrently requests a reviewer to also render an opinion of value, the reviewer should conclude the business appraisal review engagement prior to commencing the business appraisal engagement.

Note that under present USPAP professional standards, it is possible to perform a review and render an opinion of value concurrently. I do not recommend that you ever do so, as such an arrangement can potentially be seen as a conflict of interest.

PREPARING A DOCUMENT REQUEST FOR A REVIEW ENGAGEMENT

A reviewer should keep in mind that the scope of an appraisal review engagement is determined by the appraisal process undertaken by the appraiser, the engagement facts and circumstances, *and* the reviewer's informed judgment.

Remember, it is you, as the reviewer, who determines the nature and extent of the scope for your review. However, the information requested should be sufficient for you to develop a foundation for the review opinion that you will be providing. In other words, as a reviewer, you need to also climb your own Credibility Pyramid.

Thus, the documents and information that may be requested by a reviewer should be relevant to these attendant issues. While the appraisal report is the first item to be obtained, the scope of a review engagement may extend to facts and circumstances not included or that failed to be considered during the appraisal process that is undertaken by the appraiser. By way of illustration, the following are examples of categories of documents, facts, and circumstances that a reviewer may wish to consider as part of the information to be requested:

- Copy of the signed appraisal report, together with all exhibits.
- Copy of the executed appraisal engagement agreement.
- All correspondence exchanged between the appraiser and the client, including document requests issued by the appraiser during the course of the appraisal engagement.
- If the appraisal review is part of an ongoing litigation, the reviewer may wish to request a listing of the items produced during discovery and select from this list the items determined relevant by the reviewer.
- An attempt should be made to request access to the appraiser's work file.
- Carefully read the appraisal report's statement of limiting conditions and assumptions and request support for relevant engagement-specific issues that are listed.
- Carefully read relevant forecasting assumptions that are presented and request support for positions taken (such as growth assumptions, cap levels, etc.).
- Read the sources of information relied on by the appraiser and request support for any items considered relevant and material.
- If possible, inquire about the internal review process used by the appraiser; be on the lookout for an internal review process where more than one individual materially contributed to the final opinion of value but did not sign the appropriate appraisal certification.

- Contact professional organizations that have accredited the appraiser to ascertain the accuracy and status of the accreditations listed.
- Whenever possible, the reviewer should request a personal interview with the appraiser. If an interview is not granted, the reviewer should document any other reasonable attempts he or she made to communicate with the appraiser. The content of these communications should be determined at the discretion of the reviewer.
- Whenever feasible, the reviewer should consider requesting a site visit or taking steps to obtain information to confirm observations, statements, or conclusions pertinent to any site visit(s) performed by the appraiser.
- If a personal interview, a site visit, or access to the appraiser's work file is not possible, the reviewer may consider these, individually or collectively, to be material limitations of scope and, if so, may determine whether they should be included as part of the statement of relevant limiting conditions and assumptions.

 ## THE ROLE TO BE ASSUMED: REVIEWING EXPERT OR REVIEWING CONSULTANT

A reviewer should clearly define his or her role from the inception of a review engagement. Reviewers may also be expected to provide supporting information concerning various issues to the engaging attorney, which may impair a reviewer's independence when rendering an opinion.

As a review consultant, your role might be:

- Impeach the opposing appraiser.
- Assist the attorney in evaluating the case.
- Prepare your report if you are a testifying witness.
- Prepare the attorney for deposition and/or cross-examination.

As an opining reviewer, your role might be:

- Governed by the applicable rules of civil procedures that apply to any other testifying expert; therefore, you should seek the advice and support of legal counsel.
- If in a litigation setting, in most instances, you will be deposed by opposing counsel shortly after you submit your review or rebuttal report.
- You should be ready to stand the pressure brought on you during deposition and possibly during trial.

- Make sure that you have carefully researched all of your arguments, and you should be able to articulate them effectively and credibly.

There are other factors of which you should be aware that may be different from a traditional appraisal:

- The importance of your engagement memo, especially in areas dealing with a reviewer's independence.
- Information produced during the discovery process that was not included in the appraiser's original report, but that you may need to consider as part of your review scope.
- The effect of information in the report under review versus information introduced by an opposing expert or witness.
- A reviewer or a rebuttal expert who was either not part of legal discovery or not present in the appraiser's original report.

LIMITING CONDITIONS AND ASSUMPTIONS

A business appraisal review report should include a statement of relevant limiting conditions and assumptions. At a minimum, regardless of the type of appraisal review opinion offered, the statement of relevant limiting conditions and assumptions should incorporate the appraisal report that is reviewed as an integral assumption underlying the review opinion that is proffered:

- Information, estimates, and opinions contained in this appraisal review report were obtained from sources represented to be reliable. However, I (we) assume no liability for the accuracy of such information.
- Possession of this report or a copy thereof, does not carry with it the right of publication of any part of it, nor may it be used for any other purpose than as stated in Section X of this report.
- This appraisal review engagement is limited to the production of this report, conclusions, and opinions contained herein. The reviewer has no obligation to provide future appraisal review services. The reviewer is not required to give testimony in court or to attend any hearings or depositions.
- This appraisal review engagement is valid only for the specified purpose and intended for use only by the client, its financial advisers, tax preparers, and the Internal Revenue Service in connection with the purpose stated in Section X of this report.

- The reviewer has assumed that there is full compliance with all applicable federal, state, and local regulations and laws, unless otherwise specified in this report.
- This report was prepared under the sole direction of the reviewer. Neither the professional who worked on this engagement nor any employees of the reviewer have any present or contemplated future interest in the client or the appraiser nor any personal interest with respect to the parties involved or any other interest that might prevent the reviewer from performing an unbiased business appraisal review.
- The reviewer's compensation is not contingent on an action or an event resulting from the analyses, opinions, or conclusions in, or the use of, this report.
- Payment of all fees billed by the reviewer shall be a mandatory condition precedent to suit by the client.
- Reviewer is not a law firm, and none of its members are licensed to practice law in any jurisdiction.
- All documents provided to the reviewer are known to be originals or true copies of the originals.
- The appraisal report prepared by the appraiser dated [appraisal report date] was relied on by the reviewer to represent the appraiser's opinion of value of [the described subject interest], and it is incorporated herein as an integral part of this business appraisal review report.
- The appraiser did not perform any subsequent analysis, amendments, or changes to the [appraisal report] dated [date of appraisal certification].
- The appraiser has not given any testimony in court, depositions, hearings, or proceedings of any type regarding any matters in the appraisal report.
- The appraiser is not subject to any disciplinary actions or proceedings in connection with his or her appraisal practice or the subject matter contained in the appraisal report.

 ## DETERMINING AN APPROPRIATE SCOPE FOR YOUR REVIEW

A reviewer's opinion should encompass the business appraisal methods and procedures used by the individual whose work product is undergoing the business appraisal review. However, the scope of a business appraisal review may also include all aspects of the relationship between the appraiser and the original retaining entity. A reviewer may consider not only the appraiser's work product but also any facts, circumstances, or events that were considered or that the appraiser failed to consider, which might affect the opinion of value offered by the appraiser.

The scope of a business appraisal review should be sufficient to provide a reviewer with a basis for rendering a credible business appraisal review opinion regarding the relevance, reliability, completeness, and reliable application of the business appraisal methodology under review and its consistency with generally accepted appraisal practices in the United States.

The analysis and review methodology used by a reviewer should be determined on the basis of the requirements promulgated under the professional standards applicable to the development of the review opinion:

- A reviewer's informed judgment regarding the pertinent facts and circumstances applicable to the review engagement should be probative and supportive of the assertions stated in the appraisal review opinion.
- A user's ability to replicate a reviewer's results is also directly related to the sufficiency of the data, assumptions, and explanations presented in a business appraisal review report.
- The application of informed judgment applies to the review process, as well as to the appraisal process undertaken by an appraiser.

In developing his or her business appraisal review procedures and subsequently assessing the resulting foundational conclusions, a reviewer should consider the development and application of his or her informed judgment, as well as that of the appraiser's, along the guidelines that we discussed earlier in Chapter 4:

- As an aggregate result(s) of risk assessments, valuation conclusions, summations, and approximations resulting from the appraisal process undertaken by the appraiser premised on the appraiser's application of common sense and reasonableness:
  - In light of differing interpretations of known or knowable facts.
  - Using generally accepted approaches and methodologies.

In doing so, a reviewer should carefully assess inherently subjective issues, to avoid merely substituting the opining individual's subjectivity with that of the reviewer, under the reviewer's cloak.

In many instances, the defining difference between a subjective appraisal conclusion that is lacking in foundation and an appraiser's application of informed judgment is the presence of a well-defined analytical process, allowing a stakeholder to understand the appraiser's thought process.

MINIMUM SCOPE CONSIDERATIONS IN A REVIEW ENGAGEMENT

At a minimum, a reviewer should consider making an assessment of the following nine factors:

1. Adequacy of the statement of purpose.
2. Appropriateness of the definition of value.
3. Acceptability of the appraisal methods that were used.
4. Reliability of the selected methodology.
5. Comprehensiveness of the financial analysis.
6. Assessment of the company performance that was presented versus that of industry peers.
7. Adequacy of references and support for the industry data that was used.
8. Relevance and credibility of the value conclusion.
9. Conformance with valuation standards.

The previous factors are in addition to any other matters that a reviewer would consider to be appropriate, given the facts and circumstances of a review engagement.

When Changes in the Scope or Nature of a Review Engagement Become Necessary

In the event that a reviewer's intended scope is limited, the reviewer, in his or her own informed judgment, should make a determination regarding the sufficiency of the business appraisal review procedures that were undertaken to form a basis for the reviewer's opinion. In the event that during the course of a business appraisal review engagement, a retaining entity requests a reviewer to render an opinion of value, the reviewer should conclude the business appraisal review engagement prior to commencing the business appraisal engagement.

CONCLUSION OF A BUSINESS APPRAISAL REVIEW ENGAGEMENT

Prior to the conclusion of a business appraisal review engagement in which an appraisal review opinion is to be offered, the reviewer should obtain a letter of representation from the retaining entity. At a minimum, a review report should contain the following:

- An introduction
- An opinion
- Objectives and scope of the appraisal review
- Basis and reason(s) for the opinion offered
- Appraisal review assumptions and limiting conditions
- Sources of information relied on by the reviewer
- Certification
- Exhibits
- Reviewer's curriculum vitae

Note: The use of additional elements may be appropriate if, in the opinion of the reviewer, such an inclusion would be useful to a user of the review report.

BUSINESS APPRAISAL REVIEW OPINION

In the determination of value, a business appraisal review opinion is not an opinion of value. A reviewer's findings and conclusions should be stated in the form of a signed opinion reporting the reviewer findings pursuant to this standard, as of the completion date of the business appraisal review engagement.

Types of Opinion

When performing a qualitative review, I propose that there are three types of opinions that may applicable when reporting the results of a review engagement:

1. A finding of concurrence
2. A finding of nonconcurrence
3. A finding of no opinion

Finding of Concurrence (Suggested Reporting Language)

I was retained by [name of retaining entity] to review the accompanying appraisal report prepared by [name of the appraiser] dated [date of the appraisal report].

This business appraisal review was conducted for the purpose of determining that the approaches and methodologies used by [name of the appraiser] were relevant to the objectives and purpose(s), as stated in the appraisal report prepared by [name of the appraiser], and applied on a reliable basis consistent with generally accepted appraisal practices in the United States of America as of [date of the appraisal report]. This business appraisal review did not entail the performance of an appraisal. Therefore, this business appraisal review should not be construed to be an opinion of value.

In my opinion, subject to the assumptions and limiting conditions discussed in this business appraisal review report, the opinion presented by [name of the appraiser] is credible and found to be in conformity with generally accepted appraisal practices normally relied on by business appraisers in the United States of America, as promulgated by the business appraisal standards of the [organizations accrediting the appraiser] and the Uniform Standards of Professional Appraisal Practice (USPAP).

Signature of reviewer

Typed name of reviewer; indicate certification date.

Finding of Nonconcurrence (Suggested Reporting Language)

When a reviewer's opinion is intended to indicate a finding of irrelevance, unreliability, and/or application of appraisal methodology inconsistent with generally accepted appraisal practices, a signed opinion reporting the reviewer's finding of nonconcurrence, as of the completion date of the business appraisal review engagement, pursuant to this standard should read as follows:

I was retained by [name of retaining entity] to review the accompanying appraisal report prepared by [name of the appraiser] dated [date of the appraisal report].

This business appraisal review was conducted for the purpose of determining that the approaches and methodologies used by [name of the appraiser] were relevant to the objectives and purpose(s), as stated in the appraisal report prepared by [name of the appraiser] and applied on a reliable basis consistent with generally accepted appraisal practices in the United States of America as of [date of the appraisal report]. This business appraisal review did not entail the performance of an appraisal. Therefore, this business appraisal review should not be construed to be an opinion of value.

In my opinion, subject to the assumptions and limiting conditions discussed in this business appraisal review report, the opinion presented by [name of the appraiser] is not credible and is not in conformity with generally accepted appraisal practices normally relied on by business appraisers in the United States of America, as promulgated by the business appraisal standards of the [organizations accrediting the appraiser] and the *Uniform Standards of Professional Appraisal Practice* (USPAP).

Signature of reviewer

_____

Typed name of reviewer; indicate certification date.

Finding of No Opinion (Suggested Reporting Language)

If a reviewer's scope, procedures, analysis, and/or findings are limited by any party or entity and, consequently, are otherwise deemed inconclusive, no opinion should be issued by the reviewer. Consequently, a reviewer's findings, as of the completion date of the business appraisal review engagement, pursuant to this standard should read as follows:

> I was retained by [name of retaining entity] to review the accompanying appraisal report prepared by [name of the appraiser] dated [date of the appraisal report].
>
> Due to limitations in the scope and procedures in the business appraisal review engagement, my findings were inconclusive, and, therefore, I could not form a basis for a business appraisal review opinion.
>
> Signature of reviewer
>
> _____
>
> Typed name of reviewer; indicate certification date.

Certification

A business appraisal review report should contain certification similar to the following, given by the reviewer, which should be signed and dated by the reviewer as of the date of completion of the appraisal review engagement:

I certify that to the best of my knowledge and belief:

- The facts and data reported by the reviewer and used in the review process are true and correct.
- The analyses, opinion, and conclusions in this review report are limited only by the assumptions and limiting conditions stated in this review report and are my personal, impartial, and unbiased professional analyses, opinion, and conclusions.
- I have no (or the specified) present or prospective interest in the property that is the subject of the work under review and no (or the specified) personal interest with respect to the parties involved.
- I have no bias with respect to the subject interest under review or to the parties involved with this review assignment, the appraiser, or any parties associated with any of these parties.
- My review engagement in this assignment was not contingent on developing or reporting predetermined results.
- My compensation is not contingent on an action or event resulting from the analyses, opinion, or conclusions in this review or from its use.
- My analyses, opinion, and conclusions were developed and this review report was prepared in conformity with the *Uniform Standards of Professional Appraisal Practice.*
- I have (or have not) made a personal inspection of the subject property under review.
- No one provided significant appraisal, appraisal review, or appraisal consulting assistance to the person signing this certification. (If there are exceptions, the name of each individual[s] providing appraisal, appraisal review, or appraisal consulting assistance should be stated.)

Signature of reviewer

_____

Typed name of reviewer; indicate certification date.

Departure

In the event that a reviewer departs from any applicable professional standards, the reviewer should justify such departure and clearly state the nature and effect of the departure, if any, on the reviewer's findings.

REVIEWER'S INDEPENDENCE

A reviewer should be independent with respect to all stakeholders in the business appraisal review process, including the business appraiser whose opinion is under review and the reviewer's retaining entity.

In the event that a reviewer is engaged to function not as independent reviewer but as an adviser or a consultant, he or she may serve as an advocate. In such instances, the reviewer should include a statement of departure that states that any positions taken were done so as an advocate for the client.

Your Qualifications to Review the Work of Another

Prior to accepting an engagement to perform a business appraisal review, an opining individual should judge his or her competence to complete the business appraisal review assignment.

In addition, if during the course of a business appraisal review engagement, an opining individual concludes that he or she lacks the necessary knowledge and experience to perform a credible business appraisal review, then that individual should consider withdrawing from the review engagement.

Obtaining a Representation Letter

According to PPC, a representation letter serves two important functions in a valuation engagement:[1]

1. It makes management aware of its responsibilities to provide accurate and reliable information.
2. It makes management responsible for the relevance, completeness, and accuracy of the information provided.

Prior to the conclusion of a review engagement, a reviewer should prepare a memorandum to the retaining entity outlining the material aspects of the business appraisal review engagement that were relied on by the reviewer. The representation letter should be signed and dated by the retaining entity as close to the certification date as possible.

I also use a representation memo as a mechanism to obtain the client's acknowledgment that no unresolved conflicts of interest existed that prevented me from providing an unbiased opinion.

In situations where the reviewer may not be able to obtain material representations, the reviewer should go back and reconsider the degree of reliability that can be placed on his or her opinion and to what extent it is practically possible to condition such limitations, via the statement of relevant limiting conditions and assumptions.

For practitioners who decide to use a representation letter, it is recommended that such a requirement be outlined to the retained entity in the engagement memorandum.

The authors recommend that a representation letter should include the following acknowledgments by a retaining entity:

- An acknowledgment that the reviewer acted without bias.
- An acknowledgment of the services that were not part of the review engagement.
- An acknowledgment that the review engagement is considered completed on receipt of the review report.
- An acknowledgment that all facts and information in the possession of the retaining entity were provided to the reviewer.

COMMON ERRORS AND ANALYTICAL GAPS FOUND IN VALUATION REPORTS

Error 1: Analytical gaps.

Probably the single most common appraisal reporting error that comes up during reviews falls under the category of analytical gaps.

Analytical gaps can occur when a valuation metric or conclusion rests on a fact or a set of circumstances that is not explained by whatever preceding analysis was presented.

Analytical gaps can also occur when an appraiser simply makes unsupported statements and then proceeds to build an opinion of value around them. The reviewer should be aware that an analytical gap is not to be confused with an appraiser's use of informed judgment. The use of informed judgment involves a discussion and a presentation of facts and circumstances, with the appraiser's resulting conclusion, which is perhaps resting on an appraiser's subjective thought process.

Analytical gaps are unexplained leaps of faith from a given set of facts to the respective conclusion.

Error 2: Improper identification of the interest being valued.

The appraiser fails to specify the exact interest to be appraised. He or she states it is "the common stock."

The appraiser states that the interest being appraised is a 30 percent interest, lacking full control and marketability.

The appraiser fails to disclose whether the interest is controlling or noncontrolling.

Here is a suggested way to define an interest being valued:

The appraiser was retained by Mr. F. R. Springs, president of Aircraft Parts Distributors, Inc., to estimate the fair market value of Two Thousand Four Hundred and Fifty common voting shares, representing a forty-nine percent interest, in the no par value voting common stock, the only class of stock, authorized, issued and outstanding, of Aircraft Parts Distributors, Inc., a Florida closely held "S" corporation, on a not freely marketable minority basis, valued as a single block of common stock, as of December 31, 2001 (hereafter referred to as "The Common Stock" or "Subject Interest").

Error 3: Failure to clearly state the valuation date.

A suggested technique would be:

Valuation date: December 31, 201X

My analysis considered relevant known or knowable facts and circumstances present at XYZ, Inc., as of December 31, 201X, the "valuation date."

My opinion would most likely be different if another valuation date would be used.

Error 4: Improper appraiser certification.

Failure to mention significant assistance provided by others; failure to state that the report was prepared in accordance with the business appraisal standards of a sponsoring organization.

Error 5: Improper report date.

Confusing the valuation date with the date the report was prepared.

Error 6: Failure to provide a separate and distinct "Opinion of Value" or "Conclusion of Value" section in the business valuation report to clearly and concisely state the valuation opinion.

Error 7: Improper use of business appraisal terminology.

Error 8: Failure to properly use illustrative aids.

Whenever illustrative aids, such as charts, tables, and exhibits, are used, a discussion should be provided to explain the information presented and its connection to the analytical process. Care should also be taken to clearly label and identify any illustrative aids utilized.

Error 9: Failure to document sources of information that were used in the analytical process.

Error 10: Whenever an executive summary or transmittal letter is used, all key aspects of the valuation engagement should be properly identified, such as:

- The subject interest.
- The valuation date.
- The valuation purpose.
- The standard of value and the related premise.
- Support for the selection of the standard of value.
- The level of value.
- The degree of marketability of the subject interest.
- The degree of control of the subject interest.
- The size of the interest with respect to the remaining ownership.
- The type and class of equity.

Error 11: Failure to identify the retaining entity.

Error 12: Failure to identify the name of the client.

Error 13: Failure to edit boilerplate assumptions and limiting conditions to correspond to the facts and circumstances of the engagement.

Error 14: Failure to properly analyze, assess, and describe the benefit stream to be valued in various parts of the report, such as in the financial analysis or the economic and industry analyses.

Error 15: Failure to create a nexus between the macro analysis performed at the economic and industry levels and the operations of the subject company.

Error 16: Failure to present analytical conclusions comparing the subject company to its industry peers.

Error 17: Failure to consistently assess risk factors.

Error 18: Failure to analyze working capital components and present an assessment of the adequacy of the working level as of the valuation date, in terms of its requirements to support the company's operations, as well as any possible changes contemplated by any forward-looking assumptions, forecasts, economic, or industry trends.

Error 19: Failure to assess the forward-looking impact of the forecasting assumption on the metrics existing as of the valuation date.

Error 20: Failure to assess the impact of valuation components on the final opinion of value. For example, when the value of tangible assets makes up a large portion of the value determination, but no tangible asset appraisals are obtained.

Error 21: Failure to identify intangible value drivers.

Error 22: Failure to analyze the relationship of the value drivers that were identified to the cost of capital derived in terms of their relative rates of return.

Error 23: Failure to make, explain, and derive normalization adjustments.

Error 24: Failure to consider compensation normalization adjustments on the basis of local factors and unique facts and circumstances of the engagement.

Error 25: Failure to provide an adequate conceptual definition of the methodologies used and considered.

Error 26: Failure to adequately consider the market approach.

Error 27: Failure to identify and consider control adjustments.

Error 28: Making control adjustments when the subject interest lacks the attributes to effect those adjustments.

Error 29: Failure to report on criteria that were used to make searches.

Error 30: Failure to provide sufficient informative disclosures to allow for duplication of the information that was presented.

Error 31: Failure to properly assess growth drivers.

Error 32: Failure to consider technological trends and other industry trends on capital expenditures.

Error 33: Failure to consider the effect of a given growth rate on the relationships between capital expenditures and depreciation.

Error 34: Failure to properly assess and derive net cash flow to equity holders.

Error 35: Failure to match valuation metrics to the properly associated benefit stream.

Error 36: Failure to consider the impact of forward-looking assumptions on the resources that are available as of the valuation date.

Error 37: Failure to properly derive a capitalization rate from a discount rate.

Error 38: Failure to properly assess the attending risk factors in the derivation of a discount rate.

Error 39: Failure to consider economic and industry trends on the derivation of discount rates.

Error 40: Failure to adequately explain the basis for the derivation of unsystematic factors affecting specific company risk.

Error 41: Failure to consider the impact of the derived terminal value on the total opined amount.

Error 42: Failure to consider and assess known or knowable risk factors attending to the derivation of a terminal value.

Error 43: Inclusion of subsequent events not known or knowable as of the valuation date.

Error 44: Inclusion of nonoperating assets as part of the valuation opinion.

Error 45: Failure to consider risk factors during the derivation of valuation adjustments but assessed in other parts of the analysis.

Error 46: Failure to present credible support for the derivation of valuation adjustments.

Error 47: Failure to assess a subject's facts and circumstances when making valuation adjustments and instead relying simply on databases, studies, and other external sources of information.

Error 48: Failure to include a proper valuation certification.

Error 49: Analytical gaps caused by interim periods where no financial analysis is performed or where no financial information is presented. For example, when there is a gap between a subject's last fiscal year end that is presented and the subsequent valuation date.

Error 50: Failure to disclose conflicts of interest.

Error 51: Failure to disclose previous valuation services performed for the client.

Error 52: Failure to disclose related-party transactions, such as leases, loans, and fringe benefits.

Error 53: Failure to assess the necessary adjustments to normalize related-party transactions.

Error 54: Failure to relate company-specific risk to other risks, such as industry risk.

Error 55: Failure to consider prior sales of interests in the attending subject company.

Error 56: Failure to consider the size of the block of stock to be valued.

Error 57: Failure to consider existing provisions in buy/sell agreements.

Error 58: Failure to consider provisions in governance documents and corporate agreements that have an impact on value, such as the existence of a buy-sell agreement and its attending provisions

Error 59: Failure to consider and assess the existence of goodwill and intangible assets as well as a failure to understand the nature of intangible assets comprising the value of a subject interest.

Error 60: Failure to consider the dividend capacity of the subject company.

Error 61: Failure to identify the members of management who were interviewed and who provided information that was considered and/or used in the formulation of the opined value.

Error 62: Failure to indicate whether a site visit was conducted.

Error 63: Failure to assess the operating capacity of the subject company as of the valuation date.

Error 64: Failure to perform reasonableness tests.

Error 65: Failure to discuss the applicability of Revenue Ruling 59–60 to the valuation opinion.

Error 66: Failure to discuss the applicability of the factors enumerated in Revenue Ruling 77–287 in the derivation of a discount for lack of marketability.

Error 67: Failure to describe the quality and composition of the customer base in such terms as concentrations geographically, by customers, and by product/service lines.

Error 68: Failure to identify the shareholders, respective percentage of ownership, and class of equity held as of the valuation date when valuing closely held interests.

Error 69: Failure to identify foreseeable stakeholders; for example, failure to identify the Internal Revenue Service as a user of a tax-related valuation.

Error 70: Failure to concisely and precisely synthesize the valuation analysis conclusions in the reconciliation section of the report, in terms of the quantity and quality of the data analyzed and the suitability of the selected methodology for the valuation of the subject interest.

Error 71: Failure to present an informative table of contents in the valuation report.

Error 72: Failure to present a conclusion for each major section of the analytical process.

Error 73: Failure to accept responsibility for information received and incorporated into the opined result.

Error 74: Failure to support the selection of derived valuation multiples.

Error 75: Failure to support selections of statistical indices, such as means versus medians.

 ## CONCLUSION

This chapter offered a review approach and suggested language for reporting the results of a qualitative review and general information on reviewing the work of others. In Chapter 10, I give a final overview of the methods discussed throughout this book.

 ## NOTE

1. Jay E. Fishman, Pratt, P. Shannon, et al., *PPC's Guide to Business Valuations*, vol. 2 (Forth Worth, TX: Thomson Reuters, 2012), pp. 8–48.

CHAPTER TEN

The Journey Continues

N SUMMARY, I LEAVE YOU with some parting thoughts, including

- A definition of *credibility*.
- The attributes of a credible opinion.
- The importance of an awareness of the decision-making process and the roles of stakeholders, apart from opining individuals.
- A note on generally accepted principles.
- A definition of the concept of "informed judgment."
- Suggestions for assessing your own methodology via reasonable tests.
- Suggestions for enhancing the integrity of your opinion.

 ## DEFINITION OF *CREDIBILITY*

Credibility is an inference drawn by decision makers, resulting from an understanding of a well-defined process applied to a set of facts and circumstances under consideration.

ATTRIBUTES ATTACHED TO A CREDIBLE OPINION

1. **Replication.** To be credible, your analytical work and any related developmental assumptions, conclusions, and summations must provide a path for others to follow, together with the means to replicate your work and obtain similar results. This approach to your foundational analysis should result in supportable conclusions that can be examined by anyone reviewing your work product.

2. **Relevance.** Relevance refers to the specific relationship of your analytical nexus to a particular methodology or procedure that is forming a supportive and probative basis of the opinion.

   Moreover, relevance requires that your foundational basis, in addition to being probative of your opined results, assist the stakeholder or the decision maker in resolving disputed facts or issues.

   For example, if your objective is to value a minority interest, reaching conclusions that cannot be attributed to a minority interest will cause your opinion to lack relevance and therefore stand on a flawed foundation, because such an analysis would not aid in determining the conclusion of the value of the subject minority interest, as no connection was established between the analysis made and the minority interest to be valued. Similarly, applying a discount rate derived from net cash flow to a net income–defined benefit stream would also be irrelevant.

   If the information and the analysis that you present are not relevant to the facts and circumstances of the engagement, you will not be able to form a probative foundation; thus, your work product may add nothing to the worth of your opinion. To make matters even worse, in fact, it may turn out to be speculative and prejudicial. A helpful thought is to remember that your analytical work must connect to and be supportive of your opinion and that continuing connection must be established as an integral part of your analyses as you climb the Credibility Pyramid. Once you train yourself to be aware of the need for a nexus between your analytical work and your opinion, you will be on your way to avoiding analytical gaps.

3. **Reliability.** Your opinion must be the product of reliable principles and methods, and the methods used must be demonstrated to be properly applied. Reliability may also involve reliance on sources that are established to be credible. These requirements assure that the replication criteria can be met.

In addition, your methodology needs to be supported by a proper application. Namely, the methodology must be applied following the generally acceptable norms and conventions used by other experts under similar facts and circumstances.

For example, suppose that you present a statistical analysis of a particular data set. Let's assume that your selected statistical technique is generally accepted and used by other valuation practitioners under similar circumstances. If, however, your data points were selected using judgmental sampling, rather than random sampling, your sample size may lack a statistical foundation.

Therefore, your results cannot be duplicated, and although your statistical technique was generally accepted, a departure was made when the sample was selected without a proper sampling technique, thus lacking statistical foundation.

Improper application of the procedural requirements of otherwise reliable methodologies is also a common error that can make an opinion flawed.

As it is the case with these attributes, reliability is also directly related to other attributes, such as relevancy and completeness. The reasoning is that if you included all of the relevant facts known or knowable as of the valuation date, the results that you concluded on can be consistently applied.

It is of interest to note that in the opinion presented above, in discussing reliability, the opinion also referenced another credibility attribute, that of general acceptability, when it refers to the trial judge's determination as to whether the testimony given has a reliable basis in the knowledge and experience of the relevant discipline.

4. **Reasonableness.** You should look for additional methodologies outside of your selected methods that justify your conclusions.

   Reasonableness tests should be performed prior to the formulation of your opinion; they are part of your foundational analysis, leading up to and supporting your opinion. Reasonableness tests should embrace any alternative explanations, whether supportive or contradictory to the conclusions reached beforehand. The attribute of reasonableness also requires that any methodology that is employed be tempered with the application of informed judgment.

   These reasonableness methodologies should provide a confirmatory test, separate and apart from the valuation opinion, and, in fact, these reasonableness tests need not be as generally accepted as the primary methodologies that were used as a foundation for your opinion.

5. **Generally accepted methods and procedures (general acceptability).** These consist of the approaches, related methodologies, and procedures thereunder that have been peer reviewed and exposed to publication, which can be reasonably expected to be used by appraisers regularly conducting engagements under similar facts and circumstances.

6. **Transparency.** This refers to the inclusion and assessment of all known or knowable facts and circumstances that are known to the opining individual and presented and considered without limitation.

    A transparent analytical process contains no firewalls, omissions, or inclusions of irrelevant facts to prevent a user from having access to the information under consideration.

7. **Adequate disclosures.** This refers to the requirement that the appraisal process must not only present information of all known facts and circumstances about the appraisal process undertaken, but it must also include sufficient, informative, and relevant disclosures to allow stakeholders in the appraisal process to understand the foundation of the appraiser's opinion.

8. **Nonadvocacy.** Nonadvocacy requires that you maintain a high level of objectivity in the formulation of your own independent expert opinion throughout all aspects of the process undertaken and, in particular, during the formulation and application of your informed professional judgment, as you construct the foundational analysis supporting your opinion.

9. **Completeness.** This requires that sufficient data, assumptions, and explanations are presented and described in enough detail to provide the stakeholder or the decision maker with an accurate depiction of the overall universe of transactions under consideration.

 ## SEPARATING DECISION MAKING FROM OPINING

Anyone opining before a decision maker should carefully consider separating the decision-making aspects of the endeavor from the opining process and methodologies that are employed to proffer an opinion.

Where the work of the opining individual ends, the work of the stakeholder or the decision maker begins. However, by understanding the stakeholder's decision-making process, an opining individual can be sure to introduce relevant information in the foundational process supporting the opinion.

The truth-seeking process is like a relay race, in which one runner passes on the torch to the next runner, until the race is over—that is, truth is determined. Using this analogy, an opining individual passes on to a decision maker a credible opinion, based on an appropriate foundation and grounded in a thorough analysis of the pertinent facts and circumstances.

Conversely, opining individuals should always keep in mind that the stakeholders or the decision makers run the final track of the relay race. Opining individuals must come to terms with the idea that their opinions are not the last word within any stated set of facts and circumstances, yet they are an important part of a process that should be construed to lead to the truth regarding a set of facts and circumstances.

A given opinion, by and of itself, is not the ultimate result of a decision-making process; it is a part of the relay race. Opinions typically do not exist in a vacuum, and those that do tend to have very little utility. There is a need for opining individuals to think of the process as a foundational one via our Credibility Pyramid. Furthermore, it is important to have a defined analytical process. A well-defined analytical process may well be the differentiating trait *between an expert and a lay individual.*

 ## A NOTE ON GENERALLY ACCEPTED PRINCIPLES AND PRACTICES

Generally accepted appraisal practices in the United States are the approaches, related methodologies, and procedures thereunder that have been peer reviewed and exposed to publication *and can be reasonably expected to be used by other practitioners who are regularly conducting engagements under similar facts and circumstances.* I bring this back into the discussion for you to remember. Many times, the similarity of the facts and circumstances encountered become the pivot point that achieves consensus among practitioners.

 ## A DEFINITION OF THE CONCEPT OF INFORMED JUDGMENT

The development and application of informed judgment brings together an opining individual's training and experiences in that field of expertise and the facts and circumstances encountered in solving a problem. For our purpose, informed judgment can be operationally defined as

- The aggregate result(s) of assessments, conclusions, summations, and approximations resulting from the process undertaken by an opining individual.
- Premised on the application of intellectual rigor, common sense, and reasonableness, consistent with generally accepted practices.
- Made in light of differing interpretations of known or knowable facts.
- Applied to the problem-solving process that is undertaken.
- Using generally accepted practices, applied on a basis of objectivity, reasoning, and nonadvocacy.

Hopefully, with this definition of informed judgment, a practitioner can successfully rebut a challenge of unfounded subjectivity.

 ## SUGGESTIONS FOR ASSESSING YOUR OWN METHODOLOGY—THE IMPORTANCE OF REASONABLENESS TESTS

Recall that the Credibility Pyramid requires that you formulate a set of procedures that is intended to be supportive and probative of the opinion about to be proffered as a result of your analytical process. I refer to those procedures as reasonableness tests, which I like to define as follows: Reasonableness tests are analytical procedures applied to the opined results with the objective of establishing a commonsense and logical inference, void of speculation, on which to reach a supportive and probative *assertion* of the proffered results.

 ## SUGGESTIONS FOR ENHANCING THE INTEGRITY OF YOUR OPINION

Some suggestions for enhancing the integrity of your opinion include

- Understand the credibility threshold.
- Understand the relevance and significance of the scope undertaken.
- Understand the factual analytical responsibilities that are assumed.
- Stay within your area of expertise—resist the temptation to cross over to an allied discipline. Keep the scope of your analytical process within your area of expertise.
- Conduct your analysis within the parameters of economic reality, relevant to the facts and circumstances of the engagement.

- Maintain a high level of professional skepticism and engagement awareness.
- Review your analytical process for relevance and typical common errors.
- Resist the temptation to cite case law unless you are licensed to practice law in your jurisdiction.
- Be ready to respond to ethical challenges.

I proposed a basis for a methodology that can be used to review the work of others that is applicable across many disciplines. A powerful approach to reviewing the work of another expert is to establish a clear definition of the original purpose that was intended to be fulfilled and then to construct a review methodology that is designed to assess whether the methods and procedures that were undertaken accomplished that purpose—and thereby establish whether the opinion proffered can be worthy of belief.

Remember, as a reviewer, a great way to kick off this review methodology is to ask the practitioner whose work is under review: *Did you do what you said you were going to do?* This is also a great question to ask yourself as you reflect on your own work product.

 ## CONCLUSION

Make sure that your analysis does not leave a gap that a user of your report must leap over in order to reach your conclusion(s).

If you fail to build a "bridge" between your analysis and your conclusions, your report will again be lacking in relevance. For example, you relied on market data that could not be duplicated.

- Don't pick and choose among purported facts in order to justify an opined conclusion.
- Don't forget to logically reconcile the differences between the methodologies that you used.
- Be sure that your analysis aids a reader in reaching a conclusion. Namely, your analysis must have probative value to a user. Stay away from the temptation to present large quantities of information that do not add further probative value to your opined findings.
- Strive to use data that can be authenticated.
- List all of your sources of information, always take the high road, and disclose, disclose, disclose.

A useful criterion to follow in deciding what and how much to disclose is: Would a user's conclusions change as result of a proposed disclosure or as a result of its omission?

My sincere best wishes to all of you who have taken the time to read this book. I hope that in some way the ideas I presented may help in your continuing quest to enhance your skills and your growing desire to "get it right."

Good luck! And may your opining endeavors result in credible and productive outcomes.

Sample Valuation Service Agreement for a CPA Analyst

Follow is a sample valuation service agreement for the fictitious company, Analysts, LCC.

<Dateof Memo>

<Name>

<BusinessCity> <BusinessStateProvince>

In response to your request, we are confirming to you our understanding of the terms and objectives of this proposed Agreement and the nature and limitations of the services Analysts, LLC, and Joe Smith (hereafter referred as "Analysts" "We" "we") would render under this retainer agreement (hereafter referred as "Agreement") with <Company>, federal identification number <FederalID> (hereafter referred as "Client").

Objective, Purpose, and Valuation Date

The objective of our Valuation will be to estimate the <PurposeScope>, for the purpose of assisting Client in (define purpose) purposes, as of <AsofDate>, hereafter referred as of (insert calendar date) hereafter referred as "Valuation Date."

Deliverable

The Analysts shall deliver a written Summary Valuation ("Deliverable") under the terms and conditions of this Valuation services agreement for the stated purpose.

Commencement and Completion

The Analysts propose to start the engagement no later than three days after receipt of the signed acknowledgment accompanied by the indicated retainer. Unless nonacceptance is otherwise communicated by the Client within five business days from the date of receipt of the Deliverables, acceptance of the Deliverables shall be assumed and all of the Analysts' duties and obligations respective to the Deliverable(s) shall be considered complete, and any outstanding fees and costs then to the Analysts shall be due and payable by the Client on receipt of the Deliverables.

The Analysts will put forth their best efforts to complete this engagement by the later of December 31, 20XX, or 30 business days after receipt of all information requested by the Analysts.

Definition of Specific Interest and Level of Value to Be Valued

The specific interest to be valued by the Analysts is agreed to <Interest-Valued>, as of the Valuation Date.

Standard and Premise of Value

The Client has requested that the standard of value to be applicable to this Agreement shall be <StandardofValue>. [Consider describing the salient aspects for that particular standard of value]

Therefore, a derived estimate of value will rely on a "value in use," or going concern premise. This premise assumes that the Company is an ongoing business enterprise, with no plans to liquidate, with management operating in a rational way with a goal of maximizing value over an assumed indefinite life of the enterprise. Although the Analysts' Valuation is intended to estimate value, the Analysts assume no responsibility for a seller's or a buyer's inability to obtain a purchase contract at that price.

Fee Schedule, Payment Terms, and Conditions

The Analysts' good faith estimate in the amount of $<GoodFaith-Estimate> as calculated in the "Valuation Engagement Time Summary," in the next page, indicates the total fee to complete this Agreement.

This good faith estimate is based on the Client's timely assistance and cooperation in fulfillment of the requirements of this Agreement, which shall be determined solely on the basis of the Analysts' judgment.

In the event that the Analysts encounter unforeseen issues not contemplated by this good faith estimate, the Analysts agree to promptly notify the Client in writing. On this basis, the good faith estimate for this Valuation Agreement is as follows:

An initial retainer of $<Retainer> due upon execution of this agreement	$
Fifteen days after Receipt from the Client of items requested in "Information Request Number 1," as indicated in the attached Exhibit 2 hereto, the Analysts will invoice the Client a progress payment in the amount of	$
The balance of the fee shall be paid to the Analysts on written notice of the Agreement completion to the Client, three days prior to delivery of the Deliverable	$
Total Good Faith Fee Estimate	$

[If you wish to provide a time summary of the estimated time you need to calculate the good faith estimate provided, insert it here.]

Limiting Conditions and Assumptions of the Agreement

The Valuation Report will be subject to assumptions and limiting conditions, included as an integral part of the Valuation Report, which may include the following:

1. Information, estimates, and conclusions contained in this report are obtained from sources that are considered reliable. However, the Analysts assume no liability for such sources.

2. The Client and its representatives warranted to the Analysts that all information supplied was complete and accurate to the best of their knowledge and that the financial statements provided reflected each Company's results of operations, financial condition, and cash flow in accordance with generally accepted accounting principles, unless otherwise noted, and have been accepted by the Analysts as correct without further verification. The Analysts express no opinion on that information.

3. Possession of this report, or a copy thereof, does not carry with it the right of publication of all or part of it, nor may it be used for any purpose by anyone but the Client, without the previous written consent of the Client, or us and, in any event, only with proper attribution.

4. The Analysts will not be required to give testimony in court or attend during any hearings or depositions.

5. The estimates of value presented in this report apply to this Valuation only and may not be used out of the context presented herein. This Valuation is valid only for the purpose or purposes specified herein.

6. This Valuation assumes that the company will continue to operate as a going concern, that the character of its present business will remain intact, and that the company will be competently managed and maintained by financially sound owners.

7. The Valuation contemplates facts and conditions existing as of the Valuation Date. Events and conditions occurring after that date were not considered, and the Analysts have no obligation to update the Valuation Report for such events and conditions.

8. The Analysts will assume that there is full compliance with all applicable federal, state, and local regulations and laws, unless otherwise specified in this report, and that there are no violations of any governmental entity controlling or restricting the use of the underlying assets.

9. This report was prepared under the direction of Joe Smith, Analyst. Neither the professionals who worked on this engagement nor Analysts, LLC, have any present or contemplated future interest in the Client, any personal interest with respect to the parties involved, or any other interest that might prevent us from performing an unbiased Valuation. The Analysts' compensation is not contingent on an action or event resulting from the analyses or conclusions in, or the use of, this report.

10. No investigation of titles to the property or any claims on ownership of the property by any individuals or the Company has been undertaken. Unless otherwise stated in our report, title is assumed to be clear and free of encumbrances.

11. This engagement cannot be relied on to disclose errors, fraud, or other illegal acts.

12. At their sole discretion, the Analysts may include additional assumptions and limiting conditions in the Valuation Report as a result of performing the business Valuation.

Standards of Practice and Distribution of the Valuation Report

The Analysts' analysis and the resulting Conclusion of Value will be developed pursuant to the Code of Ethics and Business Appraisal of (insert all names of applicable standard-setting organizations). In performing this

Valuation, the Analysts will be relying on the accuracy and reliability of each Company's historical financial statements, income tax returns, forecasts of future operations, or other pertinent financial data, as well as any information obtained from third parties. The Analysts will not express an audit opinion or any form of assurance on them as those terms may be defined in any applicable accountancy rules or statutes, or warrant in any way that the Company will actually attain any of the financial levels indicated therein.

At the conclusion of the engagement, the Analysts may ask the Client to sign a representation letter on the accuracy and reliability of the financial information and the relevance of material representations used by the Analysts as part of the engagement. Should any of the information provided to the Analysts later prove to be inaccurate, incomplete, negligently prepared, or misleading, the Client hereby waives all rights and defenses pertaining to the inaccurate, incomplete, negligently prepared, or misleading information.

In no event shall the results of the Valuation provided by the Analysts or any of its analysis, narratives, summaries, or conclusions presented in development of the Valuation of value be used for the purpose of avoiding federal tax penalties or promoting, marketing, or recommending to another party any transaction or matter.

The Analysts will document the results of the engagement in a written, summary report. If, for any reason, the Analysts are unable to complete the Valuation engagement or to form a basis for its Valuation of value, the Analysts will not issue a report as a result of the engagement. The Analysts shall have no responsibility to update the Valuation Report for events and circumstances that occur after the date of its issuance. The Analysts reserve the right to resign from this engagement, if in their sole discretion they determined that continuing or completing the engagement would involve a breach of ethical or professional standards.

Conflicts of Interest

The Client and the Analysts hereby acknowledge to one another that no known conflicts of interests existed between them as of the date of execution of this agreement. Furthermore, both the Analysts and the Client agree that a representation of no conflict of interest shall also be acknowledged in the Client representation letter to be executed by the Client on conclusion of this engagement. The Client and the Analysts agree that should any conflict of interest exist or develop during the course of this engagement, such conflicts will be properly disclosed and that in the event that any such conflicts of interest prevent the Analysts from rendering an unbiased Valuation of value, then in that event the Analysts shall withdraw from the engagement and no Valuation of value shall be rendered by the Analysts. Regardless, any fees then due to the Analysts shall be promptly paid to the Analysts.

Work Papers and Confidentiality

Unless you advise the Analysts otherwise, the Analysts will assume that it is your intention and expectation to establish a confidential relationship as defined under Rule 301 of the American Institute of Certified Public Accountants Code of Professional Conduct, "Confidential Client Information," and that any other applicable Accountancy Statutes concerning client confidentiality in this State will apply to this engagement unless you advise the Analysts otherwise in writing.

All work papers created by the Analysts in pursuit of this engagement shall remain the property of and in the possession of the Analysts. The Analysts will only be responsible for returning to the Client the originals of those materials, documents, and so on, provided by the Client during the course of the engagement. The work papers for this engagement constitute confidential information. However, the Analysts may be requested to make certain work papers available to designated regulatory agencies pursuant to authority given to them by law or regulation. If requested, access to such work papers will be provided under the supervision of the Analysts' personnel. On request, the Analysts may be required to provide photo copies of selected work papers to such agencies. Any such requesting agency may intend, or decide, to distribute the photo copies or information contained therein to others, including other governmental agencies, without requiring the Analysts' consent.

The work papers for this engagement will be retained for a period of XXX years from the date of the Valuation Report. If the Analysts become aware that a regulatory agency or the Client is contesting a material finding related to this Valuation Report prepared by the Analysts herein, the Analysts will contact the respective party contesting such material finding for guidance prior to destroying the work papers supporting this engagement.

Client Responsibilities

The Client is responsible for making all management decisions and performing all management functions. The Client agrees to designate an individual possessing the suitable skills, knowledge, and /or experience to act as a point of contact for this engagement. Management is also solely responsible for evaluating the adequacy and results of the services performed by the Analysts and for accepting responsibility for the suitability of all services rendered to the purpose of this engagement.

Fraud and Internal Controls

As earlier stated, Valuation services are not designed to provide assurance on internal controls or to identify any reportable conditions. Thus, a Valuation cannot provide assurance that the Analysts will become aware of any significant matters that could otherwise be disclosed in an audit. Furthermore, a Valuation engagement cannot be relied on to disclose errors, fraud, or illegal acts that may exist. However, we will inform you of any material errors, fraud, or illegal acts that come to our attention, unless they are clearly inconsequential. In addition, the Analysts assume no responsibility to identify or communicate any significant deficiencies or material weaknesses in your internal control as part of this engagement.

Reproduction of the Valuation Report

The Client agrees not to copy or reproduce the Valuation Report or any part of it in any manner or to disclose any information contained in the report to any person not named in this agreement without the express written permission of the Analysts or to use the report for any purpose other than that which is stated in this agreement. If the Client reproduces or copies any portion of the report or discloses anything contained in the report to any person or attempts to use the Valuation Report for any purpose other than that which is stated in this agreement, the Client agrees to save, defend, hold harmless, and indemnify the Analysts from any damage, costs, or legal fees for which the Analysts may become liable as a result of the Client's unauthorized reproduction or disclosure. The distribution of the report is restricted to the internal use of Management; its legal, financial, and tax advisers; and representatives of the Internal Revenue Service and, accordingly, will not be distributed to any other parties unless all applicable statutory requirements are met beforehand and the expressed permission of the Analysts is obtained in advance.

The completed Valuation Report cannot be delivered until the Analysts have collected all fees due to the Analysts. The Analysts' Valuation Report will state that the fee received by the Analysts was not contingent on the value determined by this engagement. The Analysts shall use their best efforts in the performance of this assignment and shall be entitled to full payment of all fees without regard to any ruling of any court or the ultimate use of the report in evidence or testimony of the Analysts. Any services that may be required defending our Valuation Report in litigation, including conferences, depositions, court appearances, and testimony, if required, will be paid to the Analysts by the Client at the Analysts' expert testimony rate of $375 per hour. Any fees due under this engagement are due on receipt of our invoices. In the event of nonpayment, the Analysts reserve the right to terminate their services without any further notices, and any services so terminated shall not be resumed until any and all previously billed past-due fees are paid to the Analysts. Payment of all outstanding fees is a mandatory condition precedent to the filing of any action for recovery against the Analysts. All fees are nonrefundable.

Services and Costs Not Part of This Engagement and Not Included in Our Fee Estimate

The Good Faith Fee Estimate does not include services and costs such as travel, lodging, tax advice, tax planning, forensic accounting, or auditing any data, including data contained in any document requests. The Analysts shall not be required to meet with the Board of Directors of the Client or an audit committee or to provide any investment, external audit services, or tax planning advice to the Client.

The Analysts are not a law firm, and none of their members are licensed to practice law in any jurisdiction. Any issues considered during the course of this engagement will be considered from a layperson's perspective, using the reasoning expressed or implied within the report, unless specific written instructions given by the Client's appointed legal counsel are received by the Analysts prior to the completion of this engagement. Accordingly, our Valuation Report would not constitute a legal opinion, nor may it be relied on by any party as such. The Analysts' general descriptions should not be considered a substitute for a reader's review of the full text of any related legal documents with the aid and consultation of qualified legal counsel.

Settlement of Disputes

Payment of all fees due and billed by the Analysts shall be a mandatory condition precedent to the settlement of any disputes whether by mediation, by arbitration, or by the filing of any actions against the Analysts.

In the event of a dispute involving the interpretation or application of this agreement or the performance of the services described herein, it is agreed that such disputes shall be first referred for mediation to the American Arbitration Association. In the event that mediation is not successful at resolving any such disputes, it is agreed to submit such unresolved matters to binding arbitration under the laws of the state of Florida. In any action arising out of this agreement, the prevailing party shall be entitled to recover reasonable costs and all attorneys' fees associated with the bringing or the defense of the action. The term "costs" shall include, but not be limited to, the Analysts' time in assisting in the defense of such action, which shall be reimbursed to the Analysts at the rate of $XXX.XX per hour.

Indemnification

[Consult with your legal counsel to develop appropriate language.]

Site Visits

The Client agrees to facilitate one or more site visit(s) and make available to the Analysts any requested members of management designated by the Analysts for interviews and inquiries. Any travel costs incurred by the Analysts in connection with any site visits shall be paid by the Client.

Privacy Policy

Please refer to attached Exhibit I for the Analysts' Privacy Policy Disclosures.

Engagement Team

This engagement shall be under the supervision of Joe Smith, Analyst.

Entire Agreement

This agreement sets forth the entire understanding between the parties and describes the services to be performed by the Analysts. Any additional services that the Analysts are requested to perform shall be authorized in writing and signed by both parties and will be subject to additional fees, terms, and conditions.

Time Is of the Essence

Unless the Analysts receive the indicated retainer, together with a duly executed "Acknowledgment," no later than three business days from the date of this memo, all terms, fees, and conditions indicated in this Agreement shall be null and void.

Acknowledgment and Time for Acceptance

Please indicate your understanding and acceptance of these terms and conditions for the rendering of the services outlined under this Agreement by signing and returning to us the enclosed acknowledgment.

A copy of this memo is attached for your records.

Acknowledgment Memo

The above terms and conditions are understood and accepted effective, by my signature below; the Client acknowledges that the undersigned are duly authorized to execute this agreement on behalf of the Client, and is authorizing the Analysts, LLC, to render the services outlined above.

The Client understands that the Analysts will not accept this Agreement until receipt by the Analysts of the indicated retainer $<Retainer> accompanied by the signed acknowledgment below. Furthermore, the Analysts reserve the right to discontinue rendering these services under this Agreement in the event of nonpayment of fees as required by this Agreement.

It is the intent of this agreement that all materials, documents, or information created or provided to or by the Analysts shall be held to be Confidential.

The fees contemplated herein do not include costs such as travel, meals, and lodging or services associated with the preparation of financial statements, amendments of tax returns, goodwill impairment testing, compiling, reviewing or auditing any data, including data contained in any document requests issued by the Analysts. Any additional services requested to be rendered by the Analysts shall be requested in writing by the Client and shall be billed separately on the basis of the Analysts' customary schedule of fees and paid by the Client, as follows:

Principal	$XXX per hour
Senior staff analyst	$XXX per hour
Staff analyst	$XXX per hour
Word processing, proofreading, and report reproduction	$XXX per hour

During the course of this Agreement, the Analysts will be relying on the accuracy and reliability of historical financial statements, income tax returns, and/or other pertinent documents or financial data provided by the Client or the Client's Counsel. However, the Analysts will not express an opinion or any form of assurance on them, nor warrant or vouch for any of the operating results or financial condition that may be indicated therein. The Analysts' services are not intended to disclose errors, fraud, or illegal acts.

Accepted by:

_____

Name of Client Representative, Capacity,
on behalf of <Company> on this _____ of _____, 20_____

Please provide the following information for Engagement Administration Purposes:

The Name of the Designated Contact Person with suitable skill, knowledge, or experience who will be responding to any document or information requests in pursuit of the engagement: _____

Designated contact's staff position: _____

E-mail address:_____

Contact's phone number:_____

Client's confidential postal address to send any correspondence:
_____

Please provide the following information of additional individuals who will be receiving copies of the Valuation Report that the Analysts will be preparing:

Name	E-mail Address	Postal Address	Phone Number

Analysts, LLC, Privacy Policy

Analysts, similar to all providers of personal financial services, are now required by law to inform their Client of their policies regarding the privacy of Client information. Analysts have been and continue to be bound by professional standards of confidentiality that are even more stringent than those required by law. Therefore, we have always protected your right to privacy.

Types of Nonpublic Personal Information We Collect

We collect nonpublic personal information about you that is provided to us by you or obtained by us from third parties with your authorization.

Parties to Whom We Disclose Information

For current and former Clients, we do not disclose any nonpublic personal information obtained in the course of our practice, except as required or permitted by law. Permitted disclosures include, for instance, providing information to our employees and, in limited situations, to unrelated third parties who need to know that information to assist us in providing services to you. In all such situations, we stress the confidential nature of the information being shared.

Protecting the Confidentiality and Security of Client Information

We retain records relating to professional services that we provide so that we are better able to assist you with your professional needs and, in some cases, to comply with professional guidelines. In order to guard your nonpublic personal information, we maintain physical, electronic, and procedural safeguards that comply with our professional standards.

• • •

Please call if you have any questions, because your privacy, our professional ethics, and the ability to provide you with quality financial services are very important to us.

About the Author

Francisco "Frank" Rosillo, CPA, is the managing director of the Valuations and Forensics Advisory, LLC, serving an international clientele. The firm provides business valuations, mergers and acquisitions transactions, and forensic accounting advisory services. Rosillo is a frequent national lecturer and trainer in valuation and forensic accounting topics. He has authored Institute of Business Appraisers (IBA) courses and the practice aid *Business Appraisal Review.* He is a member of the board of governors of the Institute of Business Appraisers. Rosillo has been the recipient of several CPA accounting professional awards in business valuations and litigation support. His experiences as a financial expert witness include cases in federal and state courts.

Index